PATRICK
IN HIS OWN WORDS

JOSEPH DUFFY

VERITAS

First published 2000 by
Veritas Publications
7-8 Lower Abbey Street
Dublin 1

Reprinted 2001

ISBN 1 85390 525 9

British Library Cataloguing
in Publication Data.
A catalogue record for
this book is available
from the British Library.

With special thanks to:
Pádraig Ó Baoighill who prepared the Irish translation

'Confessio' and 'Epistola ad Milites Corotici' reproduced from *The Book of Letters of Saint Patrick the Bishop* by David Howlett, with kind permission of Four Courts Press, Dublin.

Designed by Bill Bolger
Printed in the Republic of Ireland by Betaprint Ltd, Dublin

Veritas books are printed on paper made from the wood pulp of managed forests. For every tree felled, at least one tree is planted, thereby renewing natural resources.

CONTENTS

INTRODUCTION

There are several good reasons for a new edition of 'Patrick in his own words', published initially in 1972 and reprinted many times since then.

The first is to introduce Patrick to a new generation of potential readers. His account of his life is without question one of the most remarkable stories in Irish history, full of compelling drama and adventure. It is also one of the great classics of our Christian tradition with a timeless and universal message which deserves to be kept available in the most accessible form.

Perhaps for modern readers the great asset of these writings is their brevity. It was as if Patrick foresaw the difficulty we have these days to find a few minutes to sit down and read. Everything relates directly and immediately to the message. The Confession, the longer of the two writings, is an overview of his Christian life in terms of his conversion, vocation and mission and in the light of serious and damaging charges made against him by his fellow-clergy in his native Britain. The Letter to the soldiers of Coroticus, on the other hand, is a sharp denunciation of a British prince who had raided his mission and brutally killed some of his converts.

Patrick's method in his Confession is to describe a series of key incidents in his life which he saw as God's direct intervention. This intervention came mostly by way of dreams which made such a profound impression on him that he could recall them vividly at the end of his life and put them into their context. He was so convinced of the truth of these experiences that he saw them as defining moments which gave meaning and direction to his life.

There is a growing demand today for more sharing of faith from direct personal experience. This is the area where Patrick has much to offer. When he wrote his Confession, his faith-life had reached maturity: it was solidly grounded in Scripture and the creeds of the early Church and fully integrated into the ups and downs of daily life. For him his Christian life was his real life; when he spoke about Christ he was speaking honestly and humbly about himself and this comes through in his writing. The story of his life as he tells it unfolds the great universal themes of the Christian life: his appreciation of and total dependence on God's grace, his radical conversion of heart, his response to God's call at different critical times in his life, his total and unremitting dedication to his ministry.

Apart from giving his account as accurately as possible, Patrick's main concern is to convince his readers. He is fully aware that his visions have to meet rigorous criteria if they are to be believed. This means including details which show him at a disadvantage, for example, admitting personal faults which were embarrassing. He sets out the facts of his life for his contemporaries and invites them to judge the truth of his story for themselves.

Only in recent years has the exceptional quality of Patrick's self-discernment been acknowledged. His difficult and concentrated style tends to obscure an intimate familiarity with Biblical and Patristic culture and a shrewd sensitivity to the political realities in which he found himself. Mention must also be made of the priority he gave to consecrated religious life which is difficult to explain unless he had some personal experience of the kind of monastic community described in the biographies of Martin of Tours and Germanus of Auxerre.

Patrick comes across as a caring pastor who was also a prophet with the courage to move into new pastures. The Letter to the soldiers of Coroticus burns with inconsolable heartache and deeply felt rage at the fate of his converts: in the Confession he stubbornly refuses to take a well-earned rest in order to protect his consecrated virgins. For a man of intense passion and iron commitment he has many endearing human qualities. He never underestimates the agonising demands of faith, he feels the isolation from home and family, he is patient with the weakness of the flesh.

For the reader who wants to follow Patrick more closely and, perhaps, consult his original Latin, which is provided here in an appendix, a few reminders may be in order. Patrick did not write in Classical Latin but in Late or Vulgar Latin, of which there are virtually no other surviving samples from fifth-century Britain or Ireland. The outstanding achievement of the distinguished Austrian scholar, Ludwig Bieler, in the 1940s and '50s was to identify and study in depth this form of Patrick's Latin. Despite his work, however, and that of his successors in the field, we still cannot be certain of the precise meaning of several words and phrases. This means in practice that the translator often comes between Patrick and his modern reader.

There is also the use of Christian terminology. While, as we have seen, Patrick's work is intensely personal and was certainly not composed as a teaching manual, he expresses himself in the style and language of the Bible and the Church of the fifth century. Recent studies have shown evidence of his acquaintance with the writings of the great Latin Fathers. He was also keenly aware of the Church law of the day. In fact, not only the Letter to the soldiers of Coroticus, which was a formal letter of excommunication, but the Confession itself was born out of the experience of an ecclesiastical trial. The details of the case against Patrick are so central to his thinking that they give us a valid basis for analysing the entire text. We have his formal introduction, the marshalling of his arguments, the flow of scriptural quotations to support the arguments, and, finally, the conclusion, followed by a postscript and a second conclusion.

Lastly, there is the thorniest question of all, the historical context and background of these writings over which so much ink has been spilled. As a fellow Monaghan man, Henry Morris, once said of Patrick's life: it's like looking at the actors without being able to see the stage. On the other hand, the controversies of the last hundred years have shed much new and interesting light at different times on various sections of that vast stage, the sets of which move freely, and often vaguely, from Britain to Ireland to the lands of the Picts and the Gauls. The temptation has always been to use Patrick to light the stage rather than to see what the stage has to tell us about Patrick. It seems better to accept that, for the present at least, parts of the stage remain unlit. But if we want to reach the real Patrick – and there is every reason why we should – we do well to give the historians their say.

In gratefully acknowledging the work of Patrician scholars over the years, and especially those mentioned in this volume, the last word goes to the general reader. Patrick is too important to be left to the scholars. He belongs to all of us, north and south of Ireland, east and west of the Irish Sea, 'even to distant parts beyond which nobody lives' (C 34).*

---

* The Confession and the Letter to the Soldiers of Coroticus are abbreviated C and L respectively, followed by numbers that refer to the traditional division of the text.

PART I

PATRICK'S WRITINGS

CHAPTER ONE

PATRICK'S WRITINGS

CONFESSION

Repaying a debt

[1] I am Patrick, a sinner, the most rustic and least of all the faithful, the most contemptible in the eyes of a great many people. My father was Calpornius, a deacon and the son of the presbyter Potitus. He came from the village of Bannaventaberniae where he had a country residence nearby. It was there that I was taken captive.

I was almost sixteen at the time and I did not know the true God. I was taken into captivity to Ireland with many thousands of people. We deserved this fate because we had turned away from God; we neither kept his commandments nor obeyed our priests who used to warn us about our salvation. The Lord's fury bore down on us and he scattered us among many heathen peoples, even to the ends of the earth. This is where I now am, in all my insignificance, among strangers.

[2] The Lord there made me aware of my unbelief that I might at last advert to my sins and turn whole-heartedly to the Lord my God. He showed concern for my weakness, and pity for my youth and ignorance; he watched over me before I got to know him and before I was wise or distinguished good from evil. In fact he protected me and comforted me as a father would his son. [3] I cannot be silent then, nor

indeed should I, about the great benefits and grace that the Lord saw fit to confer on me in the land of my captivity. This is the way we repay God for correcting us and taking notice of us; we honour and praise his wonders before every nation under heaven.

Profession of faith in the Trinity

4 There is no other God,
there never was and there never will be,
than God the Father
unbegotten and without beginning,
from whom is all beginning,
holding all things as we have learned;
and his son Jesus Christ
whom we declare
to have been always with the Father
and to have been begotten spiritually by the Father
in a way that baffles description,
before the beginning of the world,
before all beginning;
and through him are made all things, visible and invisible.
He was made man,
defeated death
and was received into heaven by the Father,
who has given him all power over all names
in heaven, on earth, and under the earth;
and every tongue should acknowledge to him
that Jesus Christ is the Lord God.
We believe in him
and we look for his coming soon
as judge of the living and of the dead,
who will treat every man according to his deeds.
He has poured out the Holy Spirit on us in abundance,
the gift and guarantee of eternal life,
who makes those who believe and obey

sons of God and joint heirs with Christ.
We acknowledge and adore him
as one God in the Trinity of the holy name.

Reasons for writing

5 He himself has said through the prophet: *Call upon me in the day of your trouble; and I will deliver you, and you shall glorify me.* He also says: *It is honourable to reveal and confess the works of God.* 6 Although I am imperfect in many ways I want my brothers and relatives to know what kind of man I am, so that they may perceive the aspiration of my life. 7 I know well the statement of the Lord which he makes in the psalm: *You will destroy those who speak falsely.* He says again: *A lying mouth destroys the soul.* The same Lord says in the Gospel: *On the day of judgement men will render account for every careless word they utter.* 8 I ought therefore to dread with fear and trembling the sentence of that day when no one will be able to escape or hide, but when all of us will have to give an account of even our smallest sins before the court of the Lord Christ.

9 For this reason I long had a mind to write, but held back until now. I was afraid of drawing general gossip on myself because I had not studied like the others who thoroughly imbibed the law and theology, both in equal measure. They never had to change their medium of speech since childhood but were able rather to improve their mastery of it while I, on the other hand, had to express myself in a foreign language. Anyone can easily see from the flavour of my writing how little training and skill in the use of words I got. As Scripture says: *Through the way he expresses himself shall the wise man be discerned, and his understanding and knowledge and instruction in truth.*

10 But what good is an excuse, no matter how genuine, especially since I now presume to take up in my old age what I failed to do as a young man? It was my sins then that prevented me from making my own of what I had read superficially. But who believes me although I should repeat what I said at the beginning?

The letter may not be elegant

I was taken captive as an adolescent, almost a speechless boy, before I knew what to seek and what to avoid. This is why I blush with shame at this stage and positively quail at exposing my lack of learning. I am unable to open my heart and mind to those who are used to concise writing in a way that my words might express what I feel. [11] If, indeed, I had been equipped as others were, I would not be silent in making my reparation. And if by chance I seem to some to be pushing myself forward, with my lack of knowledge and my slow speech, it is after all written: *The tongues of stammerers will quickly learn to speak peace.* How much more, then, must we earnestly strive, we who are, in the words of Scripture, *a letter of Christ bearing salvation to the uttermost parts of the earth?* The letter may not be elegant but it is assuredly and most powerfully written on your hearts, not with ink but with the spirit of the living God. The Spirit elsewhere is a witness that *even rustic ways have been created by the Most High.*

God's gift must be told

[12] I am, then, first and foremost a rustic, an untaught refugee indeed who does not know how to provide for the future. But this much I know for sure. Before I was humbled I was like a stone lying in the deep mud. Then he who is mighty came and in his mercy he not only pulled me out but lifted me up and placed me at the very top of the wall. I must, therefore, speak publicly in order to repay the Lord for such wonderful gifts, gifts for the present and for eternity which the human mind cannot measure.

[13] Let you be astonished, you great and small men who revere God! Let you, lords, clever men of letters, hear and examine this! Who was it who roused me, fool that I am, from among those who are considered wise, expert in law, powerful in speech and general affairs? He passed over these for me, a mere outcast. He inspired me with fear, reverence and patience to be the one who would if possible serve

the people faithfully to whom the love of Christ brought me. The love of Christ indeed gave me to them to serve them humbly and sincerely for my entire lifetime if I am found worthy.

14 My decision to write must be made, then, in the light of our faith in the Trinity. The gift of God and his eternal consolation must be made known, regardless of danger. I must fearlessly and confidently spread the name of God everywhere in order to leave a legacy after my death to my brothers and children, the many thousands of them, whom I have baptised in the Lord. 15 I am not at all worthy to receive so much grace after all the trials and difficulties, after captivity and so many years among that heathen people. The Lord, indeed, gave much to me, his little servant, more than as a young man I ever hoped for or even considered.

Daily prayer

When 16 I had come to Ireland I was tending herds every day and I used to pray many times during the day. More and more the love of God and reverence for him came to me. My faith increased and the spirit was stirred up so that in the course of a single day I would say as many as a hundred prayers, and almost as many in the night. This I did even when I was staying in the woods and on the mountain. Before dawn I used to be roused up to pray in snow or frost or rain. I never felt the worse for it; nor was I in any way lazy because, as I now realise, the spirit was burning within me.

Taking flight

17 In my sleep there indeed one night I heard a voice saying to me: 'It is well that you fast, soon you will go to your own country.' After a short while I again heard a voice saying: 'Look, your ship is ready.' It was quite a distance away, about two hundred miles; I never had been to the place, nor did I know anyone there. Shortly after that I ran away and left the man with whom I had spent six years. The

power of God directed my way successfully and nothing daunted me until I reached that ship.

18 The day I arrived the ship was set afloat and I spoke to the crew in order that I might be allowed to sail with them. But the captain was annoyed and he retorted angrily: 'On no account are you to try to go with us.' When I heard this I left them to go back to the little hut where I was lodging. On the way I began to pray, and before I had ended my prayer I heard one of them shouting loudly after me: 'Come quickly, these men are calling you.' I went back to them at once and they began to say to me: 'Come on, we will take you on trust; make your bond of friendship with us in any way you wish.' I refused on that day to suck their nipples out of reverence for God, but rather hoped they would come to faith in Jesus Christ for they were heathens. Thus I got my way with them and we set sail at once.

Food for the journey

19 After three days we came to land and for twenty-eight days we made our way through deserted country. Supplies ran out and the party was the worse for hunger. One day the captain began to say to me: 'Tell me this, Christian. You say your God is great and all-powerful; why then can you not pray for us? As you see we are in danger of starving; it is unlikely indeed that we will ever see a human being again.' I said to them confidently: 'Turn sincerely with your whole heart to the Lord my God because nothing is impossible for him, that this day he may send you food on your way until you are satisfied; for he has plenty everywhere.' And with the help of God so it happened. Suddenly a herd of pigs appeared on the road before our eyes; they killed many of them and stopped there for two nights.

They were well fed, and had their fill of pork, for many of them had grown weak and had been left half-dead along the way. After this they gave profuse thanks to God and I became honourable in their eyes. From that day they had plenty of food. They even found wild honey and offered me some. One of them said; 'This is offered in sacrifice.' Thank God, I tasted none of it.

Overcoming Satan

[20] The same night when I was asleep Satan tempted me with a violence which I will remember as long as I am in this body. He fell on me like a great rock and I could not stir a limb. How did it occur to me in my ignorance to call on Elijah? Meanwhile I saw the sun rising in the sky, and while I was shouting 'Elijah! Elijah!' at the top of my voice the brilliance of that sun fell suddenly on me and lifted my depression at once. I believe that I was sustained by Christ my Lord and that his Spirit was even then calling out on my behalf. I hope this is how it will be in my time of trouble, as he said in the Gospel. On that day, the Lord declares, *it is not you who speak, but the Spirit of your Father speaking through you.*

Final escape

[21] And so it was that, after many years, I was taken captive again. On my first night among my captors I received a divine message which said: 'You will be with them for two months.' That is just what happened. On the sixtieth night the Lord rescued me from their hands.

[22] As well as food for the journey he also gave us fire and dry weather every day until we met people ten days later. As I said above, we were in all twenty-eight days travelling through deserted country and the night we met people we had not a pick of food left.

Call of the Irish

On [23] another occasion, a few years later, I was in Britain with my relatives who welcomed me as a son and earnestly begged me that I should never leave them, especially in view of all the hardships I had endured. It was there one night I saw the vision of a man called

Victor, who appeared to have come from Ireland with an unlimited number of letters. He gave me one of them and I read the opening words which were: 'The voice of the Irish.' As I read the beginning of the letter I seemed at the same moment to hear the voice of those who were by the wood of Voclut which is near the Western Sea. They shouted with one voice: 'We ask you, holy boy, come and walk once more among us.' I was cut to the heart and could read no more, and so I learned by experience. Thank God, after very many years the Lord answered their cry.

Prayer of the Saviour

24 Another night – whether in me or beside me I do not know, God knows – I was called in the most learned language which I heard but could not understand, except for the following statement at the end of the prayer: 'He who gave his life for you, he it is who is speaking in you.' At that I awoke full of joy.

Prayer of the Spirit

25 On yet another occasion I saw a person praying within me. I was as it seemed inside my body and I heard him over me, that is, over the inner man. There he was, praying with great emotion. All the time I was puzzled as I wondered greatly who could possibly be praying inside me. He spoke, however, at the end of the prayer, saying that he was the Spirit. In this way I learned by experience and I recalled the words of the apostle: *The Spirit helps the weaknesses of our prayer; for we do not know how to pray as we ought; but the Spirit himself pleads for us with sighs unutterable that cannot be put into words.* Again: *The Lord our Advocate pleads for us.*

The supreme test

26 I was put on trial by a number of my seniors who came to cast up my sins as unfitting me for my laborious episcopate. On that day

indeed the impulse was overpowering to fall away not only here and now but forever. But the Lord graciously spared his exile and wanderer for his own name's sake and helped me greatly when I was walked on in this way. As a result I did not come out of it badly, considering the disgrace and the blame I felt. I pray God that it may not be accounted to them as a sin.

27 The charge against me which they discovered, after thirty years, was a confession which I had made before I became a deacon. In the anxiety of my troubled mind I confided to my dearest friend what I had done in my boyhood one day, in one hour indeed, because I had not yet overcome my sinful ways. God knows – I don't – whether I was yet fifteen. I did not believe in the living God, nor did I from childhood, but remained in death and unbelief until I was severely punished. I was well and truly humbled by hunger and nakedness and that every day.

28 Contrary to the case against me I went to Ireland only with reluctance and not until I was almost exhausted. All this was really to my advantage, for as a result I was purified by the Lord. He prepared me in a way which has improved me so much from my former condition that I now care and work for the salvation of others whereas then I did not even consider my own.

Final approval

29 The night following my rejection by those mentioned above, I had a vision of the night. I saw before my face a writing that dishonoured me, and simultaneously I heard God's voice saying to me: 'We have seen with disapproval the face of the chosen one deprived of his good name.' He did not say 'you have disapproved' but 'we have disapproved', as if to include himself. As he says: *He who touches you is as one who touches the apple of my eye.*

30 Thanks be to God who supported me in everything, that he did not hinder the project I had undertaken nor the task that Christ the Lord

had taught me. Rather did I feel from him no insignificant power and my good standing was approved in the presence of God and the people. [31] For these reasons I say boldly that my conscience does not reproach me here or for the future. God is my witness that I have told no lies in my account to you.

[32] My only sorrow that we should have deserved to hear such a report is for my dearest friend. To him I had confided my very soul. Before that interdiction I was told by some of the brothers that he would stand up for me in my absence. I was not there myself, nor was I even in Britain, nor did his intervention originate from me. He it was who had said to me in person; 'Look, you are going to be raised to the rank of bishop', although I was unworthy. How then did it occur to him afterwards to let me down publicly before all, good and bad, over something that he had previously granted me freely and gladly? And not he alone but the Lord also who is greater than all?

[33] Enough said. But I cannot hide the gift of God which he gave me in the land of my captivity. I sought him vigorously then and there I found him. I am convinced that he kept me from all evil because of his Spirit who lives in me and has worked in me up to this day. I am speaking boldly again. But God knows if a mere man had said this to me it may be that I would have held my tongue out of Christian charity.

Prayer of thanksgiving

[34] I give thanks to my God tirelessly who kept me faithful in the day of trial, so that today I offer sacrifice to him confidently, the living sacrifice of my life to Christ, my Lord, who preserved me in all my troubles. I can say therefore: Who am I, Lord, and what is my calling that you should cooperate with me with such divine power? Today, among heathen peoples, I praise and proclaim your name in all places, not only when things go well but also in times of stress. Whether I receive good or ill, I return thanks equally to God, who

taught me always to trust him unreservedly. His answer to my prayer inspired me in these latter days to undertake this holy and wonderful work in spite of my ignorance, and to imitate in some way those who, as the Lord foretold, would preach his Good News as a witness to all nations before the end of the world. We saw it that way and it happened that way. We are indeed witnesses that the Good News has been preached in distant parts, in places beyond which nobody lives.

Success due to God

Now [35] it would take too long to relate all my labour, item by item or even in part. Let me tell you briefly how the most gracious God often freed me from slavery; how he rescued me twelve times when my life was in danger, as well as from numerous conspiracies and things which I cannot put into words. I do not wish to bore my readers; but God, who knows all things in advance, is my witness that he used to forewarn me often by a divine message, poor orphan and ignorant as I was.

[36] How did I come by this wisdom which was not my own, I who neither knew what was in store for me, nor what it was to relish God? What was the source of the gift I got later, the great and beneficial gift of knowing and loving God, even if it meant leaving my homeland and my relatives?

[37] Many gifts were offered to me in sorrow and tears. I offended the donors and also some of my seniors against my wishes. Under the guidance of God in no way did I agree or give in to them. It was not I but the grace of God who overcame in me and resisted all those things. I came to the Irish heathens to preach the Good News and to put up with insults from unbelievers. I heard my travelling mission put down, I endured many persecutions even to the extent of chains, I gave up my free-born status for the good of others. Should I be worthy I am ready to give even my life, promptly and gladly, for his name's sake; and it is there that I wish to spend it until I die, if the Lord should grant it to me.

[38] I am very much in debt to God, who gave me so much grace that through me many people should be born again in God and afterwards confirmed, and that clergy should be ordained for them everywhere. All this was for a people newly come to belief whom the Lord took from the very ends of the earth as he promised long ago, through his prophets: *To you the nations will come from the uttermost parts of the earth and say: 'Our fathers got for themselves worthless idols, and there is no profit in them'.* And again: *I have set you to be a light for the Gentiles, that you may bring salvation to the uttermost parts of the earth.*

Duty to preach the Gospel

[39] I wish to wait there for the promise of one who never breaks his word, as he promises in the Gospel: *They will come from east and the west and sit at table with Abraham and Isaac and Jacob,* just as we believe the faithful will come from every part of the world. [40] For that reason we ought to fish well and diligently in accordance with the advice and teaching of the Lord, who says: *Follow me, and I will make you fishers of men.* There are also the words of the prophets: *Behold, I am sending fishers and many hunters, says God;* and so on.

It was then most necessary to spread out our nets so that a very great multitude might be caught for God and that there might be clergy everywhere to baptise and preach to a people in need and want. As the Lord says in the Gospel by way of exhorting and teaching: *Go therefore now, make disciples of all nations, baptising them in the name of the Father and of the Son and of the Holy Spirit, teaching them to observe all that I have commanded you; and lo, I am with you always, to the close of the age.* Again he says: *Go therefore into all the world and preach the Gospel to the whole creation. He who believes and is baptised will be saved; but he who does not believe will be condemned.* And again: *This Gospel of the kingdom will be preached throughout the whole world, as a testimony to all nations; and then the end will come.*

In the same way the Lord announces beforehand through the prophet: *And in the last days it shall be, God declares, that I will pour out my Spirit upon all flesh, and your sons and your daughters shall prophesy, your young men shall see visions, and your old men shall dream dreams; yea, and on my menservants and my maidservants in those days I will pour out my Spirit; and they shall prophesy. In Hosea he says: Those who are not my people I will call 'my people' and her who had not received mercy I will call 'her who has received mercy'. And in the very place where it was said, 'You are not my people', they will be called 'sons of the living God'.*

Fervour of Irish converts

⁴¹ How, then, does it happen in Ireland that a people who in their ignorance of God always worshipped only idols and unclean things up to now, have lately become a people of the Lord and are called children of God? How is it that the sons and daughters of Scoto-Irish chieftains are seen to be monks and virgins dedicated to Christ?

⁴² There was, in particular, a virtuous Scoto-Irish woman of noble birth and great beauty, already grown to womanhood. I had baptised her myself. A few days later she came to us with a purpose, to tell us that she had been advised, in a divine message, to become a virgin of Christ and to draw close to God. Thanks be to God, six days later she carried this out in the most excellent and enthusiastic way. So too, all the virgins. Their fathers disapprove of them, so they often suffer persecution and unfair abuse from their families; yet their number goes on increasing. Indeed, the number of virgins from our own race who were born there is beyond counting, and to these must be added the widows and those who forego their marriage rights. Of them all the women who live in slavery suffer the most. They have to endure terror and threats all the time. But the Lord has given grace to many of his handmaids and, although they are forbidden, they follow him steadfastly.

Human problems

⁴³ What if I should consider leaving them and going to Britain? How dearly would I love to go, like a man going to his homeland and

relatives, and not only there but also to Gaul in order to visit the brothers and to see the face of the saintly ones of my Lord! God knows how much I yearned for it, but I am tied by the Spirit. He makes it clear to me that if I do this he will hold me responsible for the future and I am afraid of undoing the work which I have begun. It was not really I but Christ the Lord who commanded me to come here and to stay with them for the rest of my life. The Lord willing, he will protect me from everything that is evil so that I may commit no sin against him.

44 This, I hope, is my duty, but I do not trust myself as long as I am in this mortal body. Strong is the enemy who tries every day to turn me away from the faith and purity of that true religion to which I have devoted myself to the end of my life for Christ my Lord. My uncooperative body is forever dragging me towards death, that is, towards the satisfaction of unlawful desires, and I realise this partly because I have not altogether led a life as perfect as other believers. But I confess it to my Lord and I do not blush in his sight because I am not telling lies. From the time in my early manhood when I came to know him, the love of God and reverence for him have grown in me, and up to now, by the favour of God, I have kept the faith.

45 Let him who wishes laugh and scoff. I do not intend to be silent, nor to conceal the signs and wonders that the Lord showed me many years before they happened, as befits him who knows everything, even before the beginning of time. 46 I must return unending thanks to God who often pardoned my folly and my carelessness, and on more than one occasion spared me his great wrath. Although he chose me to be his helper I was slow to accept the prompting of the Spirit. The Lord showed kindness to me a million times because he saw that I was ready, even if I did not know what to do about my position because of the number of people who were hindering my mission. They used to discuss me among themselves behind my back: 'Why does this fellow throw himself into danger among enemies who have no knowledge of God?' There was no malice on their part; they simply did not appreciate how my mission should be regarded

on account of my lack of education, and I freely admit this myself. I failed myself to realise in good time the grace that was then in me. It is obvious to me now what I should have understood earlier.

⁴⁷ Now I have given here a simple account of my brothers and fellow-servants. They believed me because of what I foretold and still foretell in order to strengthen and consolidate your faith. Would that you, too, would reach out to greater things and do better! This will be my happiness, because a *wise son is the glory of his father.*

Money matters

⁴⁸ You know, as does God, how I have behaved among you from my early manhood, with genuine faith and a sincere heart. I have equally kept faith with the heathens among whom I live and I will continue to keep it. God knows I have cheated none of them for the sake of God and his Church; nor would the thought occur to me, lest I should provoke persecution against them and against us all, or that through me the name of the Lord would be blasphemed. It is written: *Woe to the man through whom the name of the Lord is blasphemed.*

⁴⁹ Although I am unskilled in every way I have tried somehow to keep my reserve even from the Christian brethren and the virgins of Christ and the religious women who used to offer me little presents unasked. They would even leave some of their jewellery on the altar, and when I insisted on giving them back they were offended. But mine was the long-term view and for that reason I used take every precaution so that the heathens might not catch me out on any grounds of infidelity concerning myself or the work of my ministry. I was unwilling to give unbelievers even the slightest opportunity for slander or disparagement. ⁵⁰ When I baptised so many thousands, would I have expected even a penny from any of them? Tell me and I will give it back. Or when the Lord ordained through my insignificant person so many clergy and distributed the ministry to them free, did I ever ask of any of them even the price of a shoe? Speak up and I will return it.

51 On the contrary, I spent money in your interest that I might be accepted;
I travelled among you and on your account exposed myself to many
dangers everywhere, even in the most remote districts beyond which
nobody lives and where nobody had ever come to baptise, to ordain clergy
or to confirm the people. It was the Lord's gift to me that I undertook
everything with concern and eagerness for your salvation. 52 All the while I
used to give presents to the kings over and above the expenses I paid their
sons who travel with me. Even so, on one occasion they abducted my
companions and me, and were fanatically bent on killing me that day; but
my time had not yet come. They made off with everything they got their
hands on and put me in chains. Fourteen days later the Lord rescued me
from their power and our belongings were returned through the offices of
God and the good friends we had made previously. 53 You have had
experience also of how much I paid the brehons in all the districts which I
used to visit very often. I must have distributed not less than the honour-
price of fifteen men among them in order that you might have the
pleasure of my company and that I might always have the pleasure of
yours until we meet God. I do not regret this; I do not consider it enough. I
am still spending and will go on spending more. The Lord has power to
allow me ultimately to spend myself in the interest of your souls.

Purity of motive

54 Look, I called upon God to witness by my life that I am not telling
lies; that neither am I writing to you out of flattery or greed for
money, nor because I look for esteem from any of you. Sufficient is
the esteem that is not yet seen but that is felt in the heart. Faithful is
he who made the promise; he never tells a lie. 55 I see that even in this
world I have been exalted beyond measure by the Lord. Now I was
neither worthy of this nor a likely choice for the privilege.
I know perfectly well that poverty and misfortune suit me better than
riches and pleasure. Christ the Lord, himself, was poor for our sakes,
and I am myself in dire straits. Even if I wished for it I have no wealth;
nor do I pass judgement on myself in this matter, for I daily expect to
be murdered or robbed or reduced to slavery in one way or another.

Not that I fear any of these things. Because of his promises I leave myself in the hands of almighty God who rules everywhere. As the prophet says: *Cast your care upon God, and He will sustain you.*

Prayer for perseverance

56 I now entrust my soul to God, who is most faithful and for whom I am an ambassador in my humble station. For God has no favourites and he chose me for this office to become one of his ministers, even if among the least of them. 57 What return can I make to him for all his goodness to me? What can I say or what can I promise to my Lord since any ability I have comes from him? Suffice it for him to look into my heart and mind; for I am ready and indeed greatly desire it that he should give me his cup to drink, as he gave it to others who loved him. 58 My only prayer to God is that it may never happen that I should lose his people which he won for himself at the end of the earth. I ask God for perseverance, to grant that I remain a faithful witness to him for his own sake until my passing from this life. 59 If I ever did anything worth doing for my God, whom I love, I beg of him the grace to shed my blood while still with those who are also exiles and captives on his account. Though I should be denied a grave, though my corpse should be utterly torn to pieces and scattered to dogs and wild animals, though the birds of the air should devour it; I would be fully confident in this event that I had saved both body and soul. For on that day we will undoubtedly rise in the brightness of the sun, that is, in the glory of Christ Jesus our Redeemer, as sons of the living God, joint heirs with Christ and made in his image. From him and through him and for him we will reign. 60 This sun which we see rises daily at his command for our benefit, but will never reign, nor will its brilliance endure. Those who worship it will be severely punished. We, on the other hand, believe in and worship Christ the true sun who will never perish, nor will anyone who does his will. He will remain for ever as Christ remains for ever, who reigns with God the Father Almighty and the Holy Spirit before time began and now and for all eternity. Amen.

Briefly

Look, [61] I wish to explain briefly the words of my confession again and again. Before God and his holy angels I solemnly and gladly swear that I had never any motive other than the Gospel and its promises to go back to that nation from which previously I had only barely escaped.

A final request

[62] A request of those who believe and revere God. If any of you see fit to examine or to obtain this document, which has been written in Ireland by Patrick an uneducated sinner, do not attribute to me in my ignorance the little I achieved or pointed out that pleased God. Let your conclusion and the general opinion rather be the real truth, that my success was the gift of God.

This is my confession before I die.

LETTER TO THE SOLDIERS
OF COROTICUS

Patrick's right to protest

1 I, Patrick, a sinner and untaught, established in Ireland, declare myself to be a bishop. I believe most firmly that what I am I have received from God. That is why I live among uncivilised people, a stranger and exile for the love of God. He is my witness that this is so. Not that I have usually wanted to speak out in such a severe harsh way. But I am compelled by concern for God. The truth of Christ has aroused me, out of love for my neighbours and children, for whom I have given up homeland and family, and my own life even to death. If I am worthy, I live only for God to teach the heathens, even though some despise me.

2 With my own hand I have written down these words. I composed them to be related and passed on, in order that they may be sent to the soldiers of Coroticus. I do not say to my fellow-citizens or to the fellow-citizens of the holy Romans but to the fellow-citizens of the devils, because of their evil actions. In their hostile behaviour they live in death, these allies of Scoto-Irish, Picts and apostates. Dripping with blood they wallow in the slaughter of innocent Christians, whom I personally brought into the life of the baptised and confirmed in Christ.

3 The newly baptised in their white garments had just been anointed with chrism. It was still giving forth its scent on their foreheads when they were cruelly and brutally murdered, put to the sword by these men I have already mentioned. The next day I sent a letter with a holy presbyter in the company of clerics, a man I had taught from his childhood. We wanted something saved from the plunder, some of the baptised prisoners spared. They made fun of them.

Sins must be punished

4 Consequently, I do not know for whom I am to grieve the more; whether for those who were killed, for those whom they captured, or those whom the devil has deeply ensnared. Together with him they will be slaves of hell in everlasting punishment. For everyone who commits sin is a slave and is called a child of the devil. 5 Therefore, let every God-fearing person know that they are estranged from me and from Christ my God, whose ambassador I am. They are murderers of father and of brother, fierce wolves devouring the people of the Lord as they would a loaf of bread. As Scripture says: *Lord, the wicked have destroyed your law,* your law which but recently he had in his kindness successfully planted in Ireland, and which was taught by God's favour.

6 I am no usurper. My lot is with those whom he called and predestined to preach the Gospel among bitter persecutions even to the ends of the earth. I do this even though the enemy shows his jealousy through the tyranny of Coroticus, a man without respect either for God or for his priests whom he chose and graciously granted the highest form of supreme divine power, that those whom they bind on earth should be bound also in heaven.

7 So, I make these special requests of you, devout and humble-hearted men. It is not permitted to court the favour of such people, to take food or drink with them, or even to accept their alms. They must first make reparation to God through rigorous penance and in floods of tears. They must have freed the servants of God and baptised handmaids of Christ, for whom he died and was crucified.

8 The Most High rejects the gifts of the wicked. Offering sacrifice from the property of the poor is just as evil as slaughtering a son in the presence of his father. *The riches,* says Scripture, *which he gathered unjustly shall be vomited up from his belly; the angel of death drags him away; with the fury of dragons he shall be beaten; the viper's tongue shall*

slay him; unquenchable fire shall devour him. Therefore: *Woe to those who fill themselves with what is not their own.* And again: *What does it profit a man that he should gain the whole world and suffer the loss of his own soul?* ⁹ It would be tedious to discuss or to mention every single text, to gather proofs from the whole Law relating to such greed. Avarice is a deadly sin. *You shall not covet your neighbour's goods. You shall not kill.* A murderer cannot be with Christ. He who hates his brother is to be considered a murderer. *He who does not love his brother remains in death.* How much more guilty is he who has stained his hands with the blood of the children of God whom he has recently gathered at the ends of the earth through the preaching of my insignificant self?

Patrick isolated

¹⁰ Surely it was not without reference to God or for merely human purposes that I came to Ireland? Who compelled me? I am bound by the Spirit not to see any of my relatives. Surely it is not from myself that my ministry of mercy to that people derives, that people who once kidnapped me and made away with the men and women servants of my father's house? I was born free in worldly status. My father was a decurion. But I sold my noble rank without shame or regret for the benefit of others. Thus I am a servant in Christ to a far-off nation on account of the indescribable glory of eternal life which is in Christ Jesus our Lord.

¹¹ And if my own people do not recognise me, *a prophet has no honour in his own country.* Perhaps we do not belong to the same fold and do not have the same God as Father. As he says: *He who is not with me is against me, and he who does not gather with me scatters.* There is no agreement: *One man pulls down and another builds up.* I do not seek what is my own. It is not my virtue but God who put this concern into my heart that I should become one of the huntsmen or fishermen whom God once foretold would come in the last days.

Murder for money

[12] I am looked on with hate. What am I to do, Lord? I am greatly despised. Look, your sheep are torn to pieces around me and plundered by that miserable band of robbers at the bidding of the evil-minded Coroticus. Far from the love of God is the betrayer of Christians into the hands of the Scoto-Irish and the Picts. Ravenous wolves have gobbled up the flock of the Lord, which in Ireland under excellent care was really flourishing, countless sons of Scoto-Irish and the daughters of their kings having become monks and virgins for Christ. For this reason may the wrong done to the just find no pleasure with you, Lord, even as it makes its way to the depths of hell. [13] Which of the faithful would not shrink in horror from making merry or enjoying a meal with people of this sort? They have filled their houses with the spoils of dead Christians, they make their living on plunder. The wretches do not know that what they are offering as food to their friends and children is deadly poison, just as Eve did not understand that it was death she was offering her husband. So are all who do evil: by causing death they bring about their eternal punishment.

[14] This is the custom of the Christians of Roman Gaul: they send holy and suitable men to the Franks and other heathens with so many thousands of shillings to ransom baptised prisoners. But you, on the contrary, murder them and sell them to a far-off nation that does not know God. You hand over the members of Christ into what could be called a brothel. What hope have you in God, or anyone who thinks like you or converses with you in words of flattery? God will judge. For it is written: *Not only they who do evil, but also they who approve of them, shall be condemned.*

Grief and consolation

[15] I do not know what more I can say, or speak, about the departed of the children of God whom the sword struck down all too harshly. For

it is written: *Weep with those who weep.* And elsewhere: *If one member suffers, let all the members suffer with it.* Therefore, the Church mourns and laments her sons and daughters, not yet slain by the sword, but who are in exile, having been carried away into distant lands where serious and shameless sin openly abounds. Free men are sold there as slaves, Christians are reduced to slavery, and worst of all, given over to the most worthless and vilest apostates and Picts.

16 Therefore, I will cry aloud in sorrow and grief. Fairest and most dearly beloved brothers and sons, whom I begot in Christ in countless members, what can I do for you? I am unworthy to be helping either God or people. The wickedness of the wicked has prevailed over us. We have been treated like aliens. Perhaps they do not believe that we have received one and the same baptism or that we have one and the same God as Father. They think it a matter of contempt that we are Irish. Scripture says: *Have you not one God? Why have you abandoned each one of you his neighbour?*

17 Therefore, I lament for you, I lament, my dearly beloved. But again, I rejoice in my heart. I have not laboured for nothing: my travels have not been in vain. Again if this outrage, so dreadful, so unspeakable, had to happen, then God be thanked that you have left this world for Paradise as baptised Christians. I can see you: You have begun to journey where night will be no more, nor mourning nor death. But you will leap like calves freed from the tether: you will trample on the wicked and they will be like ashes under your feet. 18 You will reign with apostles and prophets and martyrs. You will receive everlasting kingdoms. As he himself testifies, saying: *They shall come from the east and from west and sit at table with Abraham and Isaac and Jacob in the kingdom of heaven. Outside shall be the dogs and sorcerers and murderers; and: As for liars and perjurers, their lot shall be in the lake of everlasting fire.* It is not without justice that the Apostle says: *Seeing that the righteous man shall only with trouble be saved, the sinner then and the impious transgressor of the law – where will he find himself?*

The sinners must repent

19 And as for Coroticus and his criminals, rebels against Christ, where will they see themselves, men who distribute young baptised women as spoil in the service of a vile earthly kingdom which may of course disappear in a moment? Like a cloud of smoke dispersed by the wind, deceitful sinners will perish when God approaches. But good men will feast with Christ without interruption, they will judge nations and they will rule over wicked kings forever and ever. Amen.

20 I testify before God and his angels that it will happen as he has indicated to me, ignorant though I may be. These are not my words which I have set out in Latin, but the words of God and of apostles and prophets: and they have never told lies. *He who believes shall be saved, but he who does not believe shall be condemned.* God has spoken.

21 Most of all I request the servant of God who will readily respond to be the bearer of this letter, that on no account should it be withdrawn or hidden from anybody, but rather that it should be read before all the communities and even in the presence of Coroticus himself. If God inspires them that at some time or other they may come to their senses again in his regard, that they may repent, even at the last minute, of their wicked crime – murder against the brothers of the Lord – and that they may free the baptised women prisoners whom they have already captured, so that they may deserve to live to God and be made well, here and in eternity, may they have peace in the Father, and in the Son, and in the Holy Spirit. Amen.

PART II

COMMENTARY AND
EXPLANATORY NOTES

CHAPTER TWO

COMMENTARY

Note
The Confession and the Letter to the Soldiers of Coroticus are abbreviated C and L respectively, followed by numbers that refer to the traditional division of the text.

HISTORICAL BEARINGS

While the Confession and the Letter to the soldiers of Coroticus contain all we know for certain about Patrick, they leave many basic questions about his life unanswered. Patrick gives no factual information other than the minimum required to describe the setting of his spiritual experiences. His rhetorical style, alternately emotional and understated, is such that we cannot be sure at times what he intends us to understand literally. Again in true Biblical fashion he refers everything in his personal life to God, almost to the total exclusion of human agents. All of these factors lead to gaps and ambiguities which are impossible to clarify from other sources. To compound the difficulties the earliest surviving copies of his writings date from at least three hundred years after their original composition. In particular, we need to keep this in mind in approaching the place-names in the text which cannot be precisely identified. Because they may be corrupt readings, they cannot support historical argument on their own.

Patrick was born a citizen of Roman Britain in its final phase, that is to say, as it gradually crumbled in the face of surrounding tribes on all sides during the fifth century. His father was a decurion or town councillor which meant that he was upper-class, well-off and part of the Roman administration. He owned a country residence with men and women servants, the place where Patrick was taken captive.

Patrick describes his boyhood as only nominally Christian even though the local clergy used to warn him about his salvation. Over the previous two centuries Christianity had come to Britain from neighbouring Gaul (present-day France) which was also part of the Roman Empire, with the same form of government and the same official language known as Vulgar or Late Latin. This is the language of Patrick's writings. Inevitably, the Church in Gaul had a lot of influence in Britain. Bishops from Gaul were regularly being invited and sent to Britain to deal with Church problems. It is significant that while Patrick's family references are to Britain, his ecclesiastical references are mainly to Gaul.

There is no consensus among scholars where Patrick's home was in Britain. Up to the nineteenth century it was thought to have been at Dumbarton on the Clyde beyond Hadrian's Wall, but this was rejected as being too far removed from Roman influence. In more recent times a location further south near Carlisle, at the extreme north of the Roman enclave, has been considered. This is the view of Charles Thomas, a foremost authority on the history of Christianity in Roman Britain. The majority of scholars, however, still opt for the general area of the Severn Valley as the place most in keeping with Patrick's comments on his Roman citizenship and his *villula*.

With many others Patrick was taken to Ireland as a slave and sent to herd livestock on the side of a mountain. Where this mountain was, has also been keenly disputed by historians. In the absence of firm evidence, modern writers tend to link it with a later reference in the Confession to the wood of Foclut, near the western sea and associated with Foghill in Killala Bay, County Mayo.

Slavery was common throughout Western Europe at this time, both inside and outside the Roman Empire. Slaves were usually prisoners of war or victims of kidnapping as Patrick was. They lost whatever human rights they had, for example, the right to marry and have a family, they were bought and sold, they were given only menial and manual work like herding livestock, which was Patrick's job, or chopping wood. In early Ireland slaves were at the bottom of a very rank-conscious society. They were also such an important element of the economy that the law strongly disapproved of their release. They had absolutely no legal protection against ill-treatment or even death at the hands of their master. In particular, the runaway slave was especially vulnerable and could not be given any protection, even by those of high rank.[1] In the light of his personal experience Patrick remained sensitive to the plight of slaves when he returned to Ireland as a missionary (C 42). He never forgot the drastic reduction in status which his own captivity brought him, the proud freeborn son of a Roman nobleman (L 10).

Apart from his religious conversion, there were positive aspects to Patrick's period of slavery in Ireland. He learned the language of the inhabitants and was able to negotiate his escape in their language. While he tells us that he spent six years with the last master he was with, his captivity may in fact have been longer than that and he may have worked in different places. It would have been impossible for Patrick to have made his highly efficient escape without a network of contacts, unknown to him personally but presumably among fellow-Christians who were already present in considerable numbers, especially in the eastern and south-eastern parts of the country. It may have been some of these who gave him shelter in the little hut where he was staying before he was allowed to board ship.

Patrick's account of his departure from Ireland and subsequent time with the crew of the ship does not flow easily as a narrative. In general it can be read as a second captivity which he was forewarned would last sixty days. This would explain the concern with counting days which is peculiar to this section. The three-day crossing by sea to his homeland is followed by twenty-eight days through the *desertum*, the uninhabited region. The first sixteen of these days ended with the food relief supplied by the stray pigs which indicated that they were getting close to people. Two days were spent resting, followed by ten with sufficient 'food, fire and dry conditions' to make the journey more tolerable. The sequence suggests a journey inland from a stormy sea into wet barren moorland and then into more wooded terrain where food was available. Eventually, after twenty-eight days, the party met up with people. Patrick does not tell us how he spent the second twenty-eight days, presumably because he had no special spiritual experiences to relate. He may have reckoned that the crew took a further twenty-eight days to do their business and to make their way back to their ship at which point he was either set free or managed to escape.

This would account for fifty-nine of the sixty days he spent in their company. Because the initiative was taken by himself, this was not so much a captivity as a form of unpleasant confinement in the company of unbelievers from whom he kept his distance. James Carney[2] has drawn attention to the fact that he uses the verb *mansi* (I remained) of his sixty days which suggests a voluntary stay (C 22). It may have to do with the agreement made when he was taken on board initially. The introductory remark 'after many years' may be a further indication that his initial captivity lasted more than six years.

The significance of the passage, apart from the two nocturnal experiences, lies entirely in its rich Biblical symbolism. As elsewhere, the historical and geographical details are played down and refer merely to a motley band of traders, or possibly pirates, who got lost somewhere in the vast tracts of mountain and forest that covered most of Britain at the time. Patrick, in recounting his journey home, not merely saw the comparison with Moses and the Exodus but told the story accordingly. Carney, who was the first to make sense of this passage, reminds us that the provision of food in the desert was a common theme in writings that would have formed an important part of the reading of the monks of Lérins, or in any part of Gaul, about this time.[3] R. Weijenborg,[4] on the other hand, collected interesting parallel references in two Greek secular writings of the period but overstates his case by claiming that the entire Confession is a work of fiction which owes its existence to these Greek texts rather than being possibly, and at most partially, influenced by them.

Some years after his return home Patrick heard the voice of the

Irish in a dream (C 23), inviting him to come back among them. This was his first intimation of his missionary vocation and he tells us that it was a long time before it became a reality. But even before this dream, his family made it clear that they did not want him to leave home again. Their reason for expressing this concern was not his mission to Ireland which lay in the distant future but his need to leave home and go abroad, to pursue higher studies and prepare for the priesthood. The question is: where did he go and for how long? It is highly significant that when he came to write his Confession he puts his wish to visit the brothers in Gaul on the same plain as his desire to see his relatives in Britain (C 43).

Recent writing tends to favour the idea that Patrick studied in Gaul, thereby reversing the earlier views of Hanson and others that the poor quality of Patrick's Latin ruled out anything but the briefest period in Gaul. A penetrating essay by Michael Herren,[5] for example, on the theme of mission and monasticism in the Confession goes a long way to establishing moral certainty in this area. Herren notes that Patrick had a deep sympathy for a higher ideal of religious life of which celibacy was the principal component, and that he actively promoted this life among his Irish converts, both male and female, to the extent that the cultivation of 'virgins of Christ' was the goal closest to his heart. From this reading of the Confession (C 40-43) Herren reasonably concludes that Patrick underwent an intense monastic experience of some duration before beginning his apostolate in Ireland. He goes further and locates this experience in Gaul rather than his native Britain. In the Confession it is Gaulish Christians, rather than their British counterparts, who are singled out for favourable mention, for example, their charity in the matter of ransoming slaves (L 14).

In his lengthy treatment of monasticism it is clearly the Gauls and not the British who are uppermost in his mind. In this he is merely reflecting the reality that the monastic movement was much stronger and much more widespread in Gaul than in Britain in the final period of the Empire. The influence of the fourth-century monk-bishop, Martin of Tours, did much to set an ascetic headline for a man with Patrick's ideals and vision.

Where to locate Patrick's monastic activities more precisely within this broad picture is another matter. Eugen Ewig[6] is inclined to accept the controversial *dictum* that Patrick journeyed 'through Gaul to Italy and the islands in the Tyrrhenian Sea', meaning that he visited the famous monastery of Lérins off the coast of Cannes. Louis Gougaud[7] explains that in the fifth century the Gulf of Genoa and the part of the Mediterranean Sea along the coast of Provence were regarded as forming part of the Tyrrhenian Sea, while Rome and the south of the peninsula did not belong to Italy, as we know it. Ewig's reason for accepting the *dictum* is that it is suited to the fifth century but not to the seventh when the fame of Lérins had faded. Similarly, there is no reason to believe that Tírechán, the seventh-century biographer of Patrick, who also accepted the *dictum,* misleads us or was misled himself when he goes out of his way to attribute these words to Patrick himself, *'ut ipse dixit'*. In recent years Latin scholars[8] are also coming round to the view that the intellectual milieu of a place like Lérins is not at all incompatible with the hitherto unsuspected sophisticated and subtle overtones of Patrick's writings. None of these arguments of course prove conclusively that Patrick studied at Lérins. But they indicate that he was much more likely to have received his clerical formation in Gaul than in Britain.

There is another point to be made about Patrick's monastic interlude. A place like Lérins attracted many visitors who did not become monks.[9] Patrick may not have formally joined the community because, while he was deeply influenced by monastic life, he knew that his calling was elsewhere. He wanted to go to Ireland as a missionary and to do that he had to prepare himself for the task. In those days and for many centuries afterwards it was common practice for the abler and more intrepid clerics to travel long distances to sit at the feet of wise and holy men. A fellow-Briton and contemporary of Patrick, Faustus, was elected abbot of Lérins in 433 and became bishop of Riez in Gaul about 460[10].

Alongside the monastic influence on Patrick was the contrasting and more worldly background of his own family and social class. The value-system here was that of the Roman administration with its high respect for the rule of civil law, the order of a settled and comfortable way of life and the benefits of education. The clergy who belonged to this class, like Patrick's father and grandfather, were not necessarily celibate (C 1) and saw no point in missionary outreach beyond the boundaries of the Empire (C 46). On the other hand, they insisted on the kind of education that Patrick missed out on when he was in Ireland as a slave – what was known as rhetoric or training in Latin writing and oratory (C 9,10,13). Patrick mentions these men specifically and with sarcasm, the 'lords and clever men of letters' (C 13). They included some of his own *seniores*, the senatorial body who assisted the bishops in running the British Church and to whom Patrick was accountable when he became a cleric.

It was these men whose lack of support and eventual hostility almost destroyed Patrick in the end. They despised him for his lack of finesse and style; they considered him incompetent and disagreed with his outreach to pagans. They did their utmost to dissuade him from going, and failing that, set about undermining him throughout his difficult mission in Ireland.

Before leaving for Ireland Patrick sold his *nobilitas*, his noble rank 'for the benefit of others' (L 10). Charles Thomas[11] takes this to refer to the family inheritance which would have come Patrick's way on the death of his father who is also mentioned here. He surmises plausibly that Patrick sold this off in order to launch his mission in Ireland. This would not, however, have ruled out the need for further funding from Britain as the mission progressed. Patrick himself explains in some detail how he continued to spend large sums of money in Ireland in different ways for the benefit of his converts (C 51-53). He makes it clear that he got nothing in return. He also distinguishes carefully between the funds available to him for this purpose – *adhuc impendo et superimpendam:* 'I am still spending and will go on spending' (C 53) – and his refusal to accept anything for himself by way of gift or stipend lest it should seem in any way to compromise his integrity (C 49-50). His hypersensitivity in the matter suggests that this was one of the false charges against him that he had to answer and a reason why he wrote the Confession, that he had considerable funds at his disposal which he was accused of spending on himself. He goes out of his way to assure his readers that he lived a frugal life, that 'poverty and misfortune' suited him better than riches and pleasure, after the example of Christ the Lord (C 55).

Patrick's comments on his finances give some slight indication of the visible scale and success of his mission. He tells us that he paid out the honour-price of fifteen men to brehons for the privilege of entering their territory to visit his converts regularly (C 53). If these were the brehons of individual *tuatha* or petty kingdoms, and Fergus Kelly[12] allots one brehon for each *tuath*, it is tempting to speculate that the approximate extent of Patrick's mission was the area of fifteen *tuatha* out of the total of over one hundred and fifty in the entire country. This rough estimate would not be inconsistent with another remark of Patrick, that over the years he performed thousands of baptisms and ordained numerous clergy in Ireland (C 50). In particular, at a mature stage of his mission, he mentions a batch of newly baptised men and women who were also confirmed with chrism. On the same occasion he alludes to a priest whom he had taught from childhood (L 3, 7). Again and again Patrick expresses his admiration for the quality of his converts (C 41-2). What is perhaps less obvious was his secure grasp of the culture in which he was working. Patrick was concerned to respect fully native law and custom, unless they were contrary to the Christian gospel, and to use them for his own ends. For example, he travelled around with a retinue of the sons of the petty kings of the *tuatha*, even though it cost him money (C 52). What he does not say is that it was a shrewd way of commanding the respect due to the king himself.[13] However, it was undoubtedly Patrick's monks and nuns who were by far the greatest influence in putting down the deep roots of Christianity in Ireland and who paved the way for the adoption of monasticism as the norm of Church organisation in the century after his death (C 41-2).

Patrick was already some time on his mission in Ireland before becoming a bishop. Otherwise it would be impossible to explain his initial freedom of choice. 'Although he chose me to be his helper I was slow to accept the prompting of the Spirit' (C 46). Patrick went to

Ireland as a volunteer, presumably from his native diocese in Britain, but fully aware from his boyhood experience of all the hazards involved. He tells us that he found it extremely hard to take the ultimate step (C 26-27). But becoming a bishop was a different matter. This meant being placed in charge of the mission for life in a specific area. To be an acceptable candidate he needed, and evidently had already a proven record of service as a successful missionary (C 32). But once he was appointed there was no question of delay, no further option: he was under a strict obligation to take up his episcopal office as soon as possible and this would have been accepted even by his critics.

This distinction between Patrick's pre-episcopal and episcopal mission is confirmed, if not explicitly stated in the text itself. Sections 47-53 of the Confession are addressed directly to Patrick's Christian converts in Ireland. He reminds them that they have known him *a iuventute,* since his early manhood (C 48). According to normal usage *iuventus* denotes the age of a person between twenty and forty and under the requisite age for a bishop in the fifth century, as we shall see shortly. This means that Patrick's mission began when he was a deacon, or more probably a priest. A reason for thinking he was a priest is the invocation in the seventh-century *Book of Durrow*: *Rogo beatitudinem tuam, sancte praesbiter Patrici* (I ask your blessing, holy priest Patrick).[14]

Patrick's episcopal appointment is mentioned at the end of a much-controverted and obscure sentence in the Confession (C 32). The context is the incident he calls the *defensio*. Patrick was already a bishop at the time and was put on trial in his absence, charged with being unfit to be a bishop. The friend who let him down on this occasion was the same man who had lined him up for the episcopacy some years earlier. He was Patrick's contemporary and was also his closest confidant from the time he became a deacon. In view of his overriding influence on all these occasions and his unique stature in the eyes of Patrick, it is very likely that he was a metropolitan bishop in Britain, or at least the most senior bishop in the area where Patrick lived. Not only was he able to give personal assurance that Patrick was going to become a bishop but he actually secured his appointment. As Tarlach Ó Raifeartaigh[15] has pointed out, the key word in the text here at the end of C 32 is *indulserat* (he had granted).

The canon law procedures of the period available to us are not as helpful as we would wish. They refer to Gaul rather than to Britain although we can be sure that the rules were much the same in both places. Patrick's appointment differed from the norm in that it was for a Christian community outside the Empire and where there was a missionary situation. Christians may have been numerous enough to ask for their own bishop but the task of finding a candidate would have devolved on the community who was sponsoring the mission. When it came to the appointment, it was the bishops of the province and especially the metropolitan who had the final say, in accordance with the regulations of the Roman See[16].

Years later, in the Letter to the soldiers of Coroticus, Patrick writes as bishop of his Irish flock. He is at pains to point out that his episcopal status derives from rightful authority: 'I am no usurper', he says (L 6). In addition to his own account of how he was appointed, this explicit statement demolishes the theory sometimes advanced that Patrick was a self-appointed bishop and that his mission to Ireland was a purely personal one without a mandate from the official Church. Patrick saw the refusal of Coroticus to take him seriously as a racist problem, not as having to do with the validity of his episcopal ordination. 'They think it a matter of contempt that we are Irish' (L 16). Whatever the personal difficulties he had with the *seniores*, who were also the sponsors of his mission, Patrick lived and worked inside the boundaries of the Church and the Sacramental system of the Church. He mentions specifically baptism, confirmation, binding and by implication loosing, the altar of sacrifice and the ordination of clergy. He includes a profession of orthodox Catholic faith in the Holy Trinity (C 4). When it happened eventually that he was repudiated publicly as a bishop, his main concern in the external forum was to have his good standing restored (C 30).

At the beginning of the Letter to the soldiers of Coroticus, Patrick declares himself to be a bishop established in Ireland. It is at this point that his brief echoes that of Palladius, sent in 431 by Pope Celestine as bishop 'to the Irish believing in Christ.' Like Palladius, Patrick was appointed bishop to existing Christian communities in Ireland; but there were important differences. Palladius was evidently given no special area or region within the country. Patrick's area would also have been open to expansion; but would have specifically excluded regions evangelised by Palladius and those bishops who replaced him. The normal logic of missionary practice would suggest that Patrick went to Ireland initially as a missionary deacon or priest to open a new mission and, having proved his evangelising skills, was then appointed bishop when his sponsors were persuaded that the mission was sufficiently well-established. We know that in due course he brought the Gospel to places for the first time; he tells us as much himself (C 51). But whether he was doing this from the beginning he does not say. What is fair to assume, however, is that when he was appointed bishop he was given his own territory and did not cut across the work of other bishops in other parts of the country. This would account for his failure to mention, even by implication, not only the mysterious Palladius but any of the others like Secundinus, Auxilius or Iserninus who were also missionary bishops in Ireland in the fifth century.

In the absence of firm contemporary evidence, historians are understandably slow to identify precisely the location of Patrick's mission in Ireland. One line of enquiry is to exclude from his influence those places where Christian communities had already existed for some time, where Palladius had come 'to the Irish believing in Christ'. These places were undoubtedly in the south and south-east of the country, nearest the Roman Empire and where trading with Britain and the Continent was well established. But we are still left to account for an immense spread of territory, stretching from the north-east to the centre and the west. If we are to believe Tírechán who wrote in the seventh century, this was all Patrick's area and it is unlikely, to say the least, that Tírechán would have written without taking full account of living traditions as he inherited and discovered them. On the other hand, he was not writing a biography as we understand the term. His purpose and conclusions relate to the politics of his own time and it is only by going back and charting the evolution of these politics over the previous two centuries that it is possible to get Patrick's remit into historical perspective. Broadly speaking, the political history of *Leath Chuinn*, the northern half of Ireland, from the fifth to the seventh centuries is as follows. The dominant power in the time of Tírechán was the Uí Néill dynasty who had extended their sway from a base west of the Shannon northwards into Ulster and then, eventually, into the midlands. One of their earliest conquests had been the *tuatha* of central Ulster, the Airgialla, who in turn at an earlier stage had themselves driven eastwards the Ulaidh, the earliest recorded warriors of Ulster who had their headquarters at Eamhain Macha, near Armagh. It is within this general framework and bearing in mind the reverence of the ancient Irish for their *seanchas* and ancestral sites that we approach the problem of locating Patrick's mission in the fifth century.

The conjunction of the Picts and the *Scotti* or Scoto-Irish in the context of the fate of Patrick's converts (L 2, 12) is another link with the north of Ireland, more specifically with the north-east. With the usual scarcity of source-material available for the period, Nora Chadwick[17] has tried to follow the traces of a small contingent of Ulaidh, otherwise known as *Scotti*, from the petty kingdom of Dál Riada in the Glens of Antrim who left their home sometime in the fifth century and set up a new colony in the south-west of Scotland. In achieving this they clashed with the inhabitants of that country, the Picts, and in time ousted them from control of Argyll and the Highlands. In the fifth century however, in other words in Patrick's time, the Picts were still a powerful force north of the Forth-Clyde line and, like the *Scotti*, they were evidently in the same slave trade of which he had been himself a victim. These pagan *Scotti*, now neighbours of the Picts and living in Britain, are contrasted unfavourably with their Christian kinsfolk in Ireland who became monks and virgins of Christ (L 12).

Some years after his appointment as bishop to Ireland, and the attack sometime later on his mission by the soldiers of Coroticus, Patrick's faith was tested to the limit, as at no other time in his life. At a meeting in Britain which took the form of a legal trial, a number of the *seniores* who opposed his mission initially and persisted in their hostility down the years, succeeded in subjecting his personal life and management of his episcopal brief to a full and public scrutiny (C 32). The discussion, among other things, uncovered an adolescent misdemeanour which Patrick had made known to the man whom he had considered to be his best friend, the very man who had granted him his episcopal appointment. The *seniores* came to Ireland to confront him with this and the other charges against him (C 26). Patrick was shaken to the foundations. What hurt him most was the *volte face* of his best friend. The temptation was intense, he says, to succumb to feelings of irreparable failure and despair. Only vivid reassurances by the Lord in a vision on the following night restored his confidence. He goes on to say that the experience did not hinder his mission, that his good standing was recovered and his orthodoxy publicly approved (C 30).

The stated charge against Patrick – his boyhood sin – sounds strange to our ears but is fully consistent with the thinking on penance and the clerical discipline of the period. In the fifth century the regular private practice of the Sacrament as we know it today had not yet been introduced and the general penitential discipline of the Church was purposely public and unbending in the extreme. Clerical discipline was even more severe and must have made it very difficult to be ordained in those days. This general background is expressed in unusual detail in the *Statuta ecclesiae antiqua*, a manual for the clerical state drawn up probably by Gennadius of Marseille about 475, and thereby reasonably close to Patrick's time and place. Canon 68 of these statutes is quite explicit. The ordination of a penitent is forbidden even if he becomes a good Christian again. If after his ordination the cleric has fraudulently concealed that he has been a former penitent, he is to be deposed. Moreover, if a bishop is party to the fraud, he loses the power to ordain. Jean Gaudemet, who is the authority on the subject,[18] quotes St Augustine (+430) who saw clearly the severity of this discipline and gave the reasons for it. Besides the obvious need to encourage humility in the penitent there was a fear of insincere penitence, undertaken with the sole motive of achieving and remaining in holy orders.

This public repudiation of Patrick is at the core of the Confession. It brought to a head a campaign on the part of many people to make him resign his mission. In the beginning they tried hard to prevent him going to Ireland. His family besought him earnestly to stay at home (C 23). Then there were those who discussed him behind his back among themselves: Why does this fellow throw himself into danger among enemies who have no knowledge of God? (C 46). Their attitude was not one of malice; they genuinely considered him unfit on account of his lack of education. With all the pleadings and reproaches he tells us that he held back until he was nearly physically exhausted (C 28). Even when he came to Ireland the hostile criticism of his mission continued (C 37). At the time of the Coroticus attack he complained bitterly about the lack of support from his own people in Britain (L 11). But what happened now was of a different order and had much more serious implications for Patrick. That his former confidant turned against him was very hurtful; but it was more than the treachery of one he thought was his friend. Patrick was now deprived of his episcopal status, of his good standing. As long as he had the backing of his friend he was secure from attack; he tells us that he had known about the trial in advance but was not worried because his brothers had reassured him of his friend's support. To take a bishop to court formally required the equivalent of a synod; but if Patrick's friend was still the metropolitan bishop which he had been at the time of Patrick's appointment, he would *ex officio* have been also the president of the synod and his role absolutely crucial in a case where he had the casting vote.

Patrick gives us an indirect clue to his age at the time of his repudiation. The incident happened thirty years after the confession he had made to his close friend before he became a deacon (C 27). It seems reasonable to draw an inference here from a decretal of Pope Siricius (384-399) to Bishop Himerius of Tarragona in Spain which gives the minimum age for diaconate at thirty years, for priesthood at thirty-five and for episcopate at forty-five. Gaudemet, who has published this information, adds that the last-mentioned is confirmed from other sources.[19] This means that Patrick was at least sixty years of age when he was accosted by the *seniores* and that he could have been at least fifteen years a bishop at the time.

The incident reveals a steady stream of communication between Patrick's mission and his British sponsors. Patrick implies that he might have been at the trial himself or at least in Britain. His frequent references to the 'brothers' indicate that there was plenty of coming and going between the two islands. When he came to write the Confession, he had decided that, in order to protect his converts, he was not going to leave Ireland. While there is no reason to dispute this, his decision may also have been due to a deep sense of grievance against his fellow-countrymen, especially after the trial. On the other hand, it is likely that it would have been necessary for him to travel to Britain in order to restore his good name and standing.

Patrick tried hard to recover his reputation. The proximate reason for writing the Confession was to vindicate himself in the immediate aftermath of the trial in the eyes of all who knew him. He directs his words mainly at his own people where his reputation had been torn to shreds – his brothers and kinsfolk (C 6), his fellow-missionaries (C 47), and finally his Irish converts whom he had known since early manhood (C 48-53).

A few questions remain. How authentic are these writings? How close in time do they get to the man to whom they are attributed? The earliest manuscript containing most of the Confession is the *Book of Armagh* which dates back to 807. The earliest manuscript with both writings is in Paris and was written for a Benedictine House in the tenth century. We know that Muirchú and Tírechán who wrote separate lives of Patrick in the seventh century used the Confession. Weijenborg, already quoted,[20] is the first scholar in recent times to have seriously questioned the attribution of both writings in their entirety to Patrick. He fastens on to those parts of the text, mainly names of persons and places, that have never been successfully identified, namely, Calpornius, Potitus, Bannaventaberniae, the *desertum*, Silva Vocluti, and gives all of them a fictitious meaning.

While these points must be taken seriously and judged on their merits, and manuscript tradition is notoriously open to corruption by embellishment as well as by omission, the greatest care must be taken not to overstate the case. Both writings give us the personal history and living faith experience of the man we call Patrick.

Finally, at what stage of the fifth century was Patrick's mission in Ireland? The weight of opinion has now returned decisively to a later rather than an earlier dating. This is the 493 date for his death which had been generally accepted before Bury's mould-breaking book of 1905. A crucial factor was the survival of many of Patrick's disciples, among them Mochta of Louth, into the sixth century. Mochta, in particular, is authenticated by Adomnán, biographer of Colmcille, as follows: 'a certain stranger, a Briton and a holy man, disciple of the holy bishop Patrick, Mochta by name'. Mochta died in AD 535.

The consequences of this *floruit* for Patrick are many and far-reaching. It rules out any association with Palladius who came to Ireland in 431 and is another reason why Palladius does not feature even by implication in Patrick's writings. It equally accounts for the absence of contact with Germanus of Auxerre who had a major influence on earlier missions. It means that the north and the west were probably the last parts of the island to be visited by missionaries, which is not surprising, given their greater distance from the Continent. It also means that the process of establishing Christianity in an institutional sense was much slower than is often thought. To accept this is to have a more realistic appreciation of the task of inculturation which Patrick understood so clearly and to which he devoted his life with singular success.

For a century and a half after his own lifetime Patrick was ignored by the people he had served so faithfully. Even when we allow for the scarcity of records and the difficulty of interpreting the sources that survive, this absence of profile has a firm basis in fact and seems to have been quite deliberate. A prolific writer like Columbanus of Bangor who died in 615 never mentions him at all, even though he cites the authority of other Irish saints and refers to the mission of Palladius. There is not a word about him in the great Penitentials of the sixth and seventh centuries, nor in the *Life of Brigid* by Cogitosus. Adomnán, the famous biographer of Colmcille, refers to him only briefly as 'the holy bishop Patrick'. Both British church historians of the early period, Gildas and the Venerable Bede, pass him by in silence. At this remove it looks as if it all had to do with the cloud of adverse criticism that hung over him during his life and which blinded his contemporaries and those who came immediately after him to his enormous achievement. This has all been to our advantage. Were it not for the cloud, we would not have either the Confession or the Letter to the soldiers of Coroticus.

ORIGINS OF THE CULT

There is every reason to believe that the popular cult, as distinct from the history of Saint Patrick, also finds its ultimate source in the Confession and the Letter. No doubt there were other reasons, mainly political, why Patrick's fame grew when and where it did and why in time he eclipsed all others as the national patron of Ireland. Scholars are now re-examining the seventh-century biographies of Muirchú and Tírechán and the motivation behind their successful promotion of Patrick as a saint for the entire country. Many of the names of persons and places we still associate with Patrick are found for the first time in these two works but the works in turn derive from older source material most of which is now lost or extant only in faint and ambiguous traces. The one shining exception is the small body of writing which all agree goes back, through the medium of scribes and copyists, to Patrick himself. The Confession and the Letter are the seeds from which the cult eventually grew and remain today the only authentic criterion by which to judge expressions of the cult. What we associate with Patrick is the extraordinary Christian humility and simplicity we find in the writings. Much of the folklore and traditional customs that celebrate him have their own historical and cultural interest but more often than not fail to do justice to the man himself.

What we mean by the cult of a saint is the first consideration. We normally associate the transmission of the Christian message with word and deed. But from the beginning the association of persons and places was also crucial. Memories of Jesus and his disciples, and the places where they lived and died, extended in time to include the early martyrs and other saints. Burial places in particular became shrines, and journeys to shrines became pilgrimages. Shrines were then multiplied by the transfer of relics from one place to another, beginning with the original burial place. In western Europe there was a further development. The shrines, the holy places, became the centres of religious leadership, initially of the clerical hierarchy and then the monasteries. Far from being a surrender to superstition and naive religiosity to which it was inevitably open, this process engaged the finest minds of the Church and was subjected to constant review and reform. In time it gradually incarnated the Christian message into personal, social and cultural behaviour with a success that words alone could never achieve and that remained virtually unchallenged until the Protestant Reformation of the sixteenth century.

The origins of the cult of Patrick have been studied recently by Charles Doherty in a substantial paper entitled 'The Cult of St Patrick and the Politics of Armagh in the Seventh Century.'[1] There were many reasons why the cult was slow to develop, the main one being the absence of a known grave. As we have seen, Patrick lived and died under a cloud. He was an itinerant missionary bishop without a strong sense of residence in one place. He was also a humble man who, far from planning a monument for himself, forecast the possibility that he might not have a grave at all (C 59). The problem was an embarrassment to his first biographers, Muirchú and Tírechán, whose main objective was to use Patrick to enhance the prestige of the church of Armagh. Much as it would have suited them to do so, they did not attempt to claim the honour of Patrick's place of burial for Armagh. According to Muirchú, this honour belonged to Downpatrick but at the time of Patrick's death the Armagh men came in search of the remains. The contention almost led to war, which was only averted at the last minute through the intercession of

Patrick. This was the official version to which both Muirchú and Tírechán subscribed. It meant that Downpatrick and Armagh were among the earliest locations of the cult, with Downpatrick in the stronger position. The tradition is recorded in the notes supplementary to Tírechán and composed at a later time that, while nobody knew at the time of composition where Patrick's bones lay, his grave was at Saulpatrick, 'in a church near the sea'. Charles Doherty, who draws attention to this, remarks perceptively that this was just the kind of humble place where we would expect to find him. Sabhall means 'barn' and, according to Muirchú, was the home of a petty chief Díchu. Díchu, we are told, was a good man and was so impressed by Patrick's preaching on their first meeting that he became a believer, Patrick's first convert, and gave the saint the barn for his first church. It was of this man and his territory, known as Magh Inis or the barony of Lecale, that Muirchú writes: 'Patrick returned to the plain of Inis, to Díchu, staying there for many days and travelled around the whole plain. He favoured and loved the district, and the faith began to spread there.'[2]

Two miles from Saul is the prehistoric town of Downpatrick, which Muirchú called by its old name of Dún Lethglaisse, which name was changed to Downpatrick only after 1177 when Patrick's relics were reputedly brought there by the Somerset knight, John de Courcy. It was also at Downpatrick that the *Life of Patrick* by Jocelin, a Cistercian monk from Lancashire, was compiled in 1185. This was the most popular of all the many *Lives* and was still being copied in manuscript form in the Gaelic version at the end of the eighteenth century.

Downpatrick's arch-rival for the relics of Patrick from the beginning, as we have seen, was Armagh. Since the seventh century the honour of being recognised as Patrick's see and first in rank of all the churches of Ireland belongs to Armagh. Muirchú and Tírechán did their work so thoroughly that this claim was never challenged by any other church, with the exception of Kildare for a period. There is of course no reference of any kind to any particular church in Patrick's own writings or any limit to the area in which he felt free to

preach. For this reason the writings had to be used indirectly and
subtly. Both Muirchú and Tírechán exploited the personality
portrayed in the writings in order to enhance the primacy of their
chosen church. The result was the emergence of Patrick as the pre-
eminent saint who became the national patron. An important
landmark here was the famous hymn in honour of St Patrick, *Audite
Omnes*, which was composed in the sixth or seventh century.
Doherty[3] has noted the echoes with the Confession as follows.
Patrick's humility is referred to (line 29), also his laborious episcopate
(line 31), he despises all worldly glory (line 53), he collects the choice
talents of Christ's Gospel when he collects with usury from the Irish
heathens (line 17-18). Colman Elo, who is the most likely author, was
a native of Antrim but became Abbot of Lynally near Durrow in
County Offaly.

As Patrick's fame travelled into the midlands and Leinster in the
seventh century, something else happened which has had important
repercussions for the cult of Patrick in our own time. The first
recorded mission to Ireland, as we know, was led by Palladius and not
by Patrick. Palladius disappeared rather suddenly from the scene but
left records of his earlier life, particularly at Auxerre in Gaul, which
were in fact more detailed than those of Patrick. While scholars were
always able to distinguish the two men in the records, in terms of the
cult and in the popular mind it was different. The more powerful cult
of Patrick, reinforced immeasurably by the two writings, absorbed
that of his rival and the two were fused into one to the advantage of
Patrick over Palladius. This amalgamation of the *acta* of the two,
Palladius and Patrick, happened as early as the seventh century, aided
and abetted by Muirchú and Tírechán, and continued to be the
accepted reading of Patrick's life until the twentieth century. Only in
the 1940s, when the work of scholars began to get general publicity,
was the true distinction restored but this time at Patrick's expense.
Initially the result was a lot of anger and confusion, at what people
saw as the unwarranted demolition of the story they had learned in
their schooldays. This was followed by the new mood of scepticism
of the 1960s and 1970s, which questioned the basic relevance of all

medieval saints to the needs of Christians in the late twentieth century. There is no doubt, however, that in the long term the cult of Patrick can only benefit by the sustained and painstaking researches of scholars. There has arguably been more serious attention given to Patrick and his writings over the past half-century than at any other period or indeed to any other personality in Irish history.

Both Muirchú and Tírechán identified the area of Slemish mountain in the south-west corner of County Antrim as the place of Patrick's captivity.[4] By the time they wrote, Slemish had already become a place of pilgrimage. In Patrick's time the lower slopes of Slemish were well wooded with fir and pine; today their strong thick roots are buried in the bog on the eastern side of the mountain. Local farmers maintain that Patrick tended only sheep on the mountain itself, that pigs and cattle would have been confined to the lower slopes. Patrick mentions 'woods' and then 'mountain' in the singular (C 17). Both Muirchú and Tírechán refer to the rock of Skerry, three miles north-east of Slemish, across the valley of the Braid, where the angel placed his foot after speaking to Patrick. Muirchú adds: 'That place is a place of prayer, and there the faithful obtain most happily the things for which they pray.' Tírechán outlines the cult of Patrick in his own time as follows:

> The holy bishop Patrick is entitled to a fourfold honour from all monasteries and churches throughout Ireland, that is:
>
> 1. On the feast of his *dormitatio* (falling asleep in death), to be honoured in the midst of Spring (i.e. Lent) for three days and three nights with every good food except meat, as if Patrick in person had come to the door.
> 2. His proper Mass to be offered on that same day.
> 3. To chant his hymn during that whole time.
> 4. Always to chant his Gaelic canticle.

The reference to 17 March is an indication of the antiquity of that feast. The hymn is taken to refer to the *Audite Omnes*, already mentioned. The Gaelic canticle is the well-known Lorica, 'I bind to myself today'. It is of special interest because, like the Confession, it is strongly Trinitarian and presupposes the existence of druidic practices. Of all the words and tunes associated with Patrick, it has the greatest popularity to the present day in its various guises, 'Christ be near at either hand' or 'Christ be beside me'.

In the popular mind the mountain most associated with Patrick is not Slemish but Croagh Patrick in County Mayo. Tírechán wrote with the Gospel story of Jesus in the desert in mind:

> And Patrick proceeded to the summit of the mountain, climbing Cruachán Aigli, and staying there forty days and forty nights... because to all the holy men of Ireland, past, present and future, God said: 'Climb, o holy men, to the top of the mountain which towers above and is higher than all the mountains to the west of the sun, in order to bless the people of Ireland' so that Patrick might see the fruit of his labours.[5]

In the Annals of Loch Cé, AD 1113, we read that 'a thunderbolt fell on Cruachán Aigle on the night of the festival of Patrick, which destroyed thirty of the fasting people'. This is an early reference to *turas na cruaiche*, the pilgrimage to the Reek every year. The Reek is the best example of how the memory of Patrick worked itself into and finally penetrated the older pagan mythology and folklore of the Irish people. A trace of the older cult has survived in the stories of Crom Dubh. In the Connacht Gaeltacht the last Sunday of July is known as Domhnach Chrom Dubh and stories tell of Patrick, more in the style of a medieval knight than of a Christian bishop, ousting Crom in the latter's abode on the mountain. Crom Dubh is sometimes identified with the more famous idol, Crom Cruaich, to whom sacrifice was offered at Samhain (1 November), which was the greatest feast of the year. By 1351, in the same Annals of Loch Cé, the Reek is called not Cruachán Aigle but Cruachán Pádruic for the first time.

During the twelfth century the pilgrimage under the patronage of Patrick to Croagh Patrick was extended to the island-shrine of Lough

Derg in County Donegal.[6] This was due to the canons regular of St Augustine who were brought to Ireland by St Malachy in 1140 and installed, among other places, on the site of an older Celtic monastery on Lough Derg. As a result of the synod of Kells in 1152 Croagh Patrick was no longer in the ecclesiastical province of Armagh and now belonged to the new province of Tuam. To make good the loss, Armagh, with the help of the canons, created a new place of pilgrimage, faithfully preserving the pilgrimage of Patrick and known ever since as St Patrick's Purgatory. About 20,000 pilgrims come here every summer to pray, fast and keep vigil for three days. Its oldest relic is a medieval stone column called St Patrick's Cross. The modern basilica (1926-31), also named after the saint, and where pilgrims keep the night part of their vigil, was the first church in Ireland or Britain with the title of basilica. It takes the place of the medieval cave where, it was claimed, Patrick was given a glimpse of purgatory, the latter being a theological development of the twelfth century which gave its distinctive name to the shrine. Like Croagh Patrick, the basic regime of prayer, fast and keeping vigil is an accurate reflection of the pilgrim life-style of Patrick as described in the Confession.

In Britain the only location of a medieval cult of Patrick was Glastonbury in Somerset. The tenth-century life of St Dunstan, abbot of Glastonbury and later archbishop of Canterbury, speaks of crowds of Irish pilgrims coming to Glastonbury to honour Patrick who was supposed to have been buried there. The same subject was pursued by William of Malmesbury who wrote between 1125 and 1130 with the help of the excellent libraries available to him at Malmesbury and nearby Glastonbury. Malmesbury was founded by an Irishman, Maeldubh, in the seventh century.[7] An interesting link between Somerset and Patrick was the Norman knight John de Courcy who brought his enthusiasm for Patrick with him from his native Stogursey (Stoke de Courcy) in Somerset to Downpatrick where he had Patrick 'buried' again. David Dumville, who has studied the question with a view to finding traces of the historical Patrick, concludes 'that, the earliest credible evidence locates a cult of Patrick at Glastonbury in the early tenth century.'[8]

Thomas F. O'Rahilly and James Carney in their day were less cautious.[9] O'Rahilly felt that the cult may go back to the monastery at Glastonbury dating from Roman times and which survived the transition from British to Saxon occupation in the seventh century. He saw this in the wider context of locating Patrick's place of capture, the mysterious Bannaventaberniae of the opening lines of the Confession. He argued that south of the Bristol Channel area was the only civilian area occupied by the Romans that was accessible to the Irish Sea and therefore vulnerable to raids from Ireland when the legions withdrew their protection in the fifth century. A further advantage of this area was its easy access to Gaul where Patrick had close personal contacts and most probably visited himself. In this connection the most recent efforts to locate Patrick's home area by a local historian Harry Jelley[10] are worthy of attention. Jelley's arguments in favour of the Somerset coast combine the place-name evidence with recent archaeological work on Roman villas in the area. He then tentatively opts for Banwell, some five miles from the modern seaside resort of Weston-Super-Mare, as the site of Patrick's place of capture. His work is a valuable gloss on Muirchú's assertion that the place 'beyond hesitation or doubt' was then Ventre and was not far from the Irish Sea.

PATRICK THE CHRISTIAN

St Patrick's Day annually focuses the attention of Irish people, at home and abroad, on their history and heritage. The saint is a national symbol, probably the only such who is acceptable to all political traditions. What tends to be overlooked is that he is much more than of Irish interest, that he deserves a wider audience. When we read his writings we discover an attractive and vulnerable personality with a memorable human story to tell. That is one of the reasons why discussion of his life continues to be open and lively and to stimulate interest and curiosity.

The question arises: how do we relate Patrick's story to the environment in which Christian faith is nourished today, as we make our way into the new millennium? We appreciate that the world Patrick looked out on was very different from our own. He came from a remote province of a decaying empire which considered the end of the world to be close at hand. He saw the Irish to be more remote still, inhabiting the edge of the world 'beyond which nobody lives'. His theological background belongs to the age of the Latin Fathers, to Augustine and Leo the Great, four times closer to the world of the New Testament than we are today. The pagan gods of his own Celtic ancestors were still alive for the people of his day, supported by a caste of druids devoted to various forms of earth worship and possessing immense influence. The Irish society that he evangelised could hardly have been more different from our own: tribal, rural, hierarchical, and family-centred as distinct from the unitary, urbanised, egalitarian and individualist society of our time.

These differences between Patrick's world and ours are replicated in the equally stark contrast between the fragmented Christian culture that he left in Britain and the vigorous if rugged pagan society he encountered in Ireland. Patrick was far from trying to bring a colonial religion to the Irish kings and princes. This is not to say that he was less than orthodox in his teaching or that he played down his Roman citizenship. But in fact Patrick's starting point had nothing to do with his cultural or social attitudes. On the other hand, it had everything to do with his own personal faith, with his perception of himself as being on intimate terms with his God in the midst of the darkness and evil around him. Patrick's God was of primary importance to him. He was not a distant and disapproving God but rather loving and accepting. The partnership between them created a dynamic harmony: Patrick accepted God's love with total trust, but he also felt accountable to God for all his actions. His concern was simply to do what was right rather than what he wanted for himself. It was this vision that enabled him to win the confidence of the people who led him into slavery. In time it came to transcend barriers of culture and creed and nation.

Patrick's journey of faith begins with the heedless frivolity of his youth. He describes a home situation familiar to many of us. There was practice of ritual without conviction, moral teaching without response, a general sense of drifting. Then without warning all changed. Short of losing his life, everything was taken, his family and friends, his community, his freedom of movement and freedom of speech, his schooling, everything we now call human rights. It was all very traumatic, very destructive of normal emotional growth and self-esteem. To the spiritual desert he had left behind was now added enforced solitude. At the age of sixteen Patrick was lost in every sense of the word, with neither friend nor future.

Why and how he turned to God in his utter misery he does not say. He may not have recalled the precise moment he crossed the threshold of prayer for the first time, or what inspired him. But he came to see it as a wonderful gift he had been given. 'When I had come to Ireland I tended herds every day and I used to pray many times during the day. More and more my love of God and reverence for him began to increase.' Implicit in the account that follows is a positive atmosphere of stillness, whether in the woods or on the mountain or in the morning before dawn. This was more than the absence of human company; it was a stillness that enabled Patrick to listen to the emotions and memories that surfaced from his own depths. In this way he got in touch with his feelings of gratitude for being alive, for having survived the ordeal of the murderous attack on his father's house. In time these feelings enabled him to confront successfully his loneliness and isolation and physical hardship. The negative feelings were also strong and deep and never left him but somehow they became secondary to God's presence. It would be naive in the extreme to underestimate the acute suffering involved or to see the daily struggle as having a predictably happy end.

There was much repetition in that early prayer of Patrick. 'My faith grew stronger,' he says, 'and my zeal so intense that in the course of a single day I would say as many as a hundred prayers, and almost as many in the night.' In other words, God hears us. But he may not answer. So we must pray again. Persistence is of the essence. All the oldest prayers like the psalms and the litanies are repetitive; they are designed to be repeated over and over again.

Without purpose, or for the wrong purpose, repetition of course leads only to tedium and frustration. On the other hand, the form and content of prayer cease to matter as long as they become a forward movement towards one's goal. The more one gets absorbed, the less overpowered one feels by cares and worries, the less disturbed by the weight of the world. Patrick had no doubt that he was preparing himself for the long haul.

As the years passed, his prayer grew in intensity. He learned to listen carefully to the promptings of his mind and to see them as coming from God, giving him the guidance he needed to make important decisions. For example, he learned to discern when the time of his captivity was coming to an end and that his ship was ready. Without the normal resources of a spiritual director or *anamchara*, he discovered within himself a power that grew with the years he spent in captivity. By the time he came to write the Confession, which was near the end of his life, he was totally saturated with a sense of God's love and care and guidance. It was God, and not himself, who was responsible for his inner happiness and fulfilment. It was God and his sense of the presence of God who controlled his movements. It was God who made his decisions.

Patrick uses different words to describe this process of allowing God to take over his life. He talks a lot about the gift of God as the overwhelming influence in his life, the incomparable gift to which all else is secondary. Because he knew that God was with him, he overcame all human fear and anxiety. He was willing to hold his ground against all comers. He was convinced that he would never be defeated or harmed where it mattered. All this in spite of being keenly aware of the enormous difficulties he had to face both from outside the fold and from within. He saw clearly the source of his strength. His only concern was to become a more fitting instrument in God's hands. He knew that his critics thought him to be deluded, too big for his boots. Because he was sensitive by nature, he was hurt by this. But he refused to be deterred. The rebuffs and setbacks he had suffered had put him outside the danger of being deluded. He had been severely humbled all his life and he knew it.

Another way in which Patrick explains the power of God at work in his life is by attributing it to the Holy Spirit. The Spirit is mentioned frequently in the Confession. Patrick is constantly 'prompted by the Spirit', 'tied by the Spirit', or 'sustained by the Spirit'. One particular vision stands out as unprecedented and possibly unique in his life. It was some time before he knew what was happening, that the Spirit was literally praying within him. We can only allow him to describe the event himself. 'On yet another occasion I saw a person praying in me. I was, as it seemed, inside my body and I heard him over me, that is, over the inner man. There he was, praying with great emotion. All the time I was puzzled as I wondered greatly who could possibly be praying inside me. He spoke, however, at the end of the prayer, saying that he was the Spirit. When I awoke I recalled the words of the Apostle: *The Spirit helps the weaknesses of our prayer; for we do not know how to pray as we ought; but the Spirit himself pleads for us with sighs unutterable that cannot be put into words* (Rom 8:26). *Again: The Lord our Advocate pleads for us* (1 Jn 2:1).

While Patrick's religious sense was intensely personal and plunged him daily into the mystery of God, his Christian commitment also found expression in practical affairs. In his relations with people his patent honesty and dedication won him loyal friends and fervent converts. He saw the importance of winning the good will and trust of the Irish chiefs and brehons. He had the normal difficulties with handling finances and was concerned to be totally accountable and transparent. He paid his staff as required by their status in society and their expenses. He was especially convinced of the value of working with young people, obviously seeing in them the white hope for the future. That the Irish Church flourished in the spectacular way it did in the period after his death was due in no small way to this wise and far-sighted policy. He was passionately concerned for the safety and welfare of his converts and all those in his care, especially the women. He refused to leave his post when it would have been normal for him to do so.

As the bishop leading the mission, Patrick had a specific job to do, a job he described himself as 'laborious' (C 26). It seems to have continually brought him into a relationship of tension with his sponsors in Britain and to have been an ongoing source of worry and pressure. He felt let down by their lack of support when his converts were taken off by the soldiers of Coroticus and did not hesitate to rebuke them publicly. He never succeeded in opening their eyes to their prejudices against the Irish and against his administration of the mission. On the other hand, their public repudiation of himself and his mission after years of hard work brought on a personal crisis of faith which nearly destroyed him. The Confession was written while the wounds inflicted by this attack on his integrity were still open and painful. Two details shed light on his inner convictions following this terrible experience. The first was his mention of his good standing being restored (C 30). This detail in many ways sums up the immediate context in which he wrote the Confession and why he needs to justify his motives and actions. Patrick was appalled at the experience of being cut off from the community of the Church and set about the process of reconciliation without delay. The second was his explicit prayer 'to shed his blood' in Ireland (C 59). In the most vivid way possible, this expresses the harmony and integration that Patrick had developed over the years between his inner communion with God and the constant physical danger to his life in which he found himself. As it turned out, he was not put to death. His martyrdom was of a different kind but it was no less real. His act of reconciliation was duly accepted and he was allowed to continue in Ireland. But there were no accolades. His mission had been declared misguided and a failure. Only well after his death did the full truth of his heroic Christian witness see the light of day.

NOTES

HISTORICAL BEARINGS

1.   Fergus Kelly, *A Guide to Early Irish Law* (Dublin, 1988), pp. 95-6; Regine Pernoud, *Martin de Tours* (Paris, 1996), p. 21.
2.   James Carney, *The Problem of St Patrick* (Dublin, 1973), p. 70.

3. Ibid., p. 73.

4. R. Weijenborg, 'Deux sources grecques de la "Confessio de Patrice"', *Revue d'Histoire Ecclésiastique'*, vol. 62 (1967), pp. 361-78.

5. Michael Herren, 'Mission and Monasticism in the *Confessio* of Patrick', in *Sages, Saints and Storytellers: Celtic Studies in Honour of Professor James Carney,* ed. Donnchadh Ó Corráin, Liam Breathnach and Kim McCone (Maynooth, 1989), pp. 76-85.

6. Eugen Ewig, 'The Missionary Work of the Latin Church', in *History of the Church,* ed. Hubert Jedin, vol. 2 (London, 1980), p. 519.

7. Louis Gougaud, *Christianity in Celtic Lands* (London, 1932, reprint, Dublin: Four Courts Press, 1992, reference to 1992 version), pp. 36-7.

8. Peter Dronke, 'St Patrick's Reading', *Cambridge Medieval Celtic Studies,* no. 1 (summer 1981), pp. 21-38; David Howlett, 'Ex saliva Scripturae Meae' (as cited in 5 above), pp. 86-101; Thomas Finan, 'The Literary Genre of St Patrick's Pastoral Letters, in *The Letters of Saint Patrick,* Daniel Conneely (Maynooth, 1993), pp. 131-150. A work that elevates Patrick's writing to a uniformly high level of artistry is D. R. Howlett's *The Book of Letters of Saint Patrick the Bishop* (Dublin, 1994), which looks set to challenge students of Latin for many years to come. Howlett's analysis has been accepted and further developed in Máire B. de Paor's *Patrick: The Pilgrim Apostle of Ireland* (Dublin, 1998).

9. Eugen Ewig, (as cited in 6 above), p. 382.

10. Elie Griffe, *La Gaule Chrétienne à l'Époque Romaine,* vol. 2, *'L'Église des Gaules au Ve siècle'* (Paris and Toulouse, 1957), p. 210.

11. Charles Thomas, *Christianity in Roman Britain to AD 500* (London, 1981), p. 332.

12. Fergus Kelly (as cited in 1 above), p. 52.

13. Ibid., p. 19.

14. Kathleen Mulchrone, 'The Mission of Patricius Secundus Episcopus Scottorum', *Irish Ecclesiastical Record,* vol. 85 (1961), p. 166.

15. Tarlach Ó Raifeartaigh, 'The Enigma of Saint Patrick', in *Seanchas Ard Mhacha,* vol. 13, no. 2 (1989), p. 46.
16. Karl Baus, 'Inner Life of the Church between Nicaea and Chalcedon', in *History of the Church* (as cited in 6 above), p. 282. See also Jean Gaudemet, *L'Église dans l'Empire Romain IVe-Ve siècles* (Paris, 1958), pp. 332-3.
17. Nora Chadwick,*The Celts* (London, 1970), pp. 88-9.
18. Jean Gaudemet (as cited in 16 above), p. 134.
19. Ibid., p. 125.
20. R. Weijenborg (as cited in 4 above), see especially pp. 363-77.

ORIGINS OF THE CULT
1. Charles Doherty, 'The Cult of St Patrick and the Politics of Armagh in the Seventh Century', in *Ireland and Northern France AD 600-850,* ed. Jean-Michel Picard (Dublin, 1991), pp. 53-94.
2. Ludwig Bieler, *The Patrician Texts in the Book of Armagh* (Dublin, 1979), p. 81.
3. Charles Doherty (as cited in 1 above), p. 91.
4. Ludwig Bieler (as cited in 2 above), pp. 83, 125.
5. Ibid., p. 153.
6. Yolande de Pontfarcy, 'The Historical Background to the Pilgrimage to Lough Derg', in *The Medieval Pilgrimage to St Patrick's Purgatory,* eds. Michael Haren and Yolande de Pontfarcy (Clogher Historical Society, 1988), pp. 32-3.
7. James F. Kenney, *Sources for the Early History of Ireland,* vol. 1, *Ecclesiastical* (New York, 1929), pp. 607-8, 226.
8. David N. Dumville, *Saint Patrick AD 493-1993* (Woodbridge, 1993), p. 240.
9. Thomas F. O'Rahilly, *The Two Patricks* (Dublin, 1942), pp. 31-34; James Carney, *The Problem of St Patrick* (Dublin, 1973), p. 122.
10. Harry Jelley, 'Locating the Birthplace of St Patrick', *British Archaeology* (July 1998), pp. 10-11.

CHAPTER THREE

EXPLANATORY NOTES

Note

The numbering of the explanatory notes refers to the section numbers in chapter one, Patrick's Writings.

CONFESSION

1 Patrick uses various words to describe church personnel: *presbyter* (C 1, L 3), *diaconus* (C 1), *episcopus* (L 1), *sacerdos* (C 1, L 6), *clerici* (C 38, 40, 51, L 3), *seniores* (C 26, 37), *monachi* (C 41, L 12), *virgines Christi* (C 41,42, 49, L 12), *sancti Domini mei* (C 43), *fratres* (C 14, 31, 43, 47, 49, L 16, 21).

The first three of these, *diaconus*, *presbyter* and *episcopus* correspond to the traditional sequence of orders in the Latin Church. *Sacerdos*, on the other hand, can be used either of *presbyter* or *episcopus* when referring to the priesthood which they have in common. *Clerici* are men either before or after ordination. *Seniores* are more difficult to explain precisely and may not refer to clergy at all. Blaise and Chirat[1] suggest a preference for a monastic meaning in C 26 but also include the meaning of elders from among the laity, 'les notables de la communauté chrétienne (sorte de conseil de fabrique)'.

Monachi, or monks, according to John Cassian who wrote during the first half of the fifth century, were Christian men who undertook an isolated and solitary life, having abstained from marriage and separated themselves from their relatives and secular affairs. In this way they could bind themselves to a common life based on the original apostolic fervour which had become weakened with the influx of converted pagans in large numbers into the Church. Communities of monks grew up where the monks lived in their own huts or cells but came together for instruction and liturgy. These were the first monasteries. The movement began in the east, in Egypt and Syria, but had spread to the Western Empire before Patrick's time. The early monks were not in clerical orders and it was only in the late fourth century that monks began to accept, often most reluctantly, the responsibilities of the priesthood and the episcopate. Both Patrick's references to monks indicate that monasticism had an important place in his model of church from the beginning although there is no reason to think that he was ever a monk himself. It is sufficient comment on his enthusiasm that the monastic movement took over in Ireland so soon and so effectively after his death.[2]

The *Virgines Christi* were women who dedicated their virginal lives exclusively to God. From the number of references alone it is clear that Patrick's female virgins were his pride and joy and that he was prepared to make any sacrifice to secure their protection, even to the extent of depriving himself of visits to Britain and Gaul to see his family and friends (C 43). They were especially vulnerable to discouragement and bullying from their parents which suggests that they remained in their own homes rather than in a convent.[3] He makes the point that Patrick's care and concern for his consecrated virgins and for their chosen vocation are totally in line with the thinking of the great writers and reformers of fifth-century western Europe, like Augustine and Pope Leo the Great. (See explanatory note 42 below.)

The *Sancti Domini mei*, like the monks and the virgins, were a special category of believers included among the more generic *fratres* or *filii Dei*. They seem to have been a religious group with whom Patrick stayed during his time in Gaul and shared a common interest, perhaps missionary outreach. *Sanctus* for Patrick, as in the early Irish Church, denotes a holy person rather than a canonised saint.

The *fratres* who are mentioned seven times throughout both writings were fellow-Christians of Patrick or simply Christians in a generic sense as in C 49 (*fratres Christiani*) or L 21 (*fratres Domini*).

2 *Dominus aperuit sensum incredulitatis meae*. Right from the start of his Confession Patrick sees God as taking the initiative in all matters of faith, beginning with his own personal conversion, extending to his theology of merit and ultimately to his theology of mission. Rather than rebutting the charges against his human inadequacies – his weaknesses and ignorance – he candidly admits these but only to show how God used him to achieve great results of which he was justly proud. Patrick's own contribution was to co-operate humbly with the Lord's will for him and he insists that he had no other motive. This mysterious relationship of divine grace with a free human response is the real drama and high tension of Patrick's story. It is also the theological theme running through the entire Confession and the Letter to the soldiers of Coroticus, and Patrick gives example after example to drive home his argument.

It is impossible to divorce Patrick's world from the Pelagian and Semi-Pelagian controversies which engaged the Latin Church in the early fifth century. In varying degrees the Pelagians sought to solve the mystery of grace by maintaining that it was a contradiction in terms to say that God could directly influence the exercise of free choice. The result was not to deny divine sovereignty but to keep God on the outside rather than at the centre of human affairs. Patrick's differences with his critics have all the signs of being part of this controversy and, while he does not say so explicitly, his theology is decisively anti-Pelagian. Why this is important is that Pelagius was himself, like Patrick, a Briton and we know from three references of Prosper of Aquitaine (413, 429 and 433) that Pelagianism had taken a strong hold in Britain and was the occasion of much dissension in the first half of the fifth century.

4 In evaluating this formal creed, Peter Dronke[4] makes more space than earlier scholars for Patrick's originality. He accepts the parallels

between Patrick and Victorinus of Pettau, a bishop and author in both Greek and Latin who lived on the borders of the Eastern and Western Empires and who was martyred probably in 303 under the Emperor Diocletian. The considerable differences, however, suggest the kind of synthesis which presupposes a familiarity on Patrick's part with the theological issues of the period after Victorinus, notably the Arian and other controversies concerning the divinity and humanity of Christ.

In the light of this it is interesting to compare Patrick's creed with the Nicean or Apostles Creed, familiar to Christians today. The central affirmation, expanded at some length, is that Jesus Christ is from eternity, 'begotten spiritually by the Father'. Not only are there no concessions here to Arius: there is no mention of the Virgin Mary or Pontius Pilate, simply that Jesus was made man and defeated death. On the other hand, in treating of the Holy Spirit, Patrick is not so heresy-conscious and is not so concerned to elaborate the divine prerogatives. He is, however, careful to state the divine personhood of the Holy Spirit, but only when he has already related the Spirit to human needs and destiny.

9 Patrick's mother tongue was Vulgar Latin which would have been mastered by him as a literary medium had he avoided captivity. While his schoolmates were being coached in Latin grammar and syntax Patrick was grappling with the foreign language of the Celtic-speaking Irish.

His demeaning of his linguistic skills, however, need not be taken too literally. After years of pouring scorn on his Latin style, scholars are now being forced to revise their views radically. This is due mainly to the work of David Howlett who has produced an entirely original and meticulously researched edition and English translation of both writings.[5] From Howlett's acute analysis Patrick emerges as an extremely self-conscious wordsmith who measured deliberately and skilfully every single word he wrote and moreover wrote to a complex and elaborate plan. The key to Patrick's style, according to Howlett, is a strict chiastic structure which makes the text easy to memorise and almost impossible to copy imperfectly. Patrick set out to compose for posterity and was primarily concerned that his work would be handed on exactly as he wrote it. He also intended at least part of his work to be read aloud (L 21).

The chiastic structure is essentially a development of the parallelism found throughout the Bible and especially in the psalms which were composed to be chanted in choir and sung in public worship. Words and phrases are repeated in such a way that they mirror each other at regular and predictable intervals and reveal balanced cross-references and complementary echoes throughout the text. Howlett however goes much further and detects more bewildering complexity. Patrick subjects his entire writing to a strict count of words, syllables and even letters, according to intricate but recognisable mosaic-like patterns. The result is not merely orderly thought but prose with a rhythm. Inevitably perhaps, there is not yet a general consensus on Howlett's work.[6]

12 With reference to Patrick's simile of the stone lying in the mud, Dronke[7] finds a close analogue in the famous *Pastor of Hermas*, the visionary text composed in Rome in the mid-second century, which was very popular in the early Church. A parable in the *Pastor* describes the building of a tower. The tower is the Church, and the stones of which it is built are the faithful. The maidens, who are blessed spirits, lift up the stones *'de profundo'*. At the Shepherd's command, even stones that are *'scabrosi'* are prepared. They are then dressed and set into the structure of the tower. But they are set in a particular order: the foundation of the tower consists of ten stones from the first age, the next twenty-five stones are from the second age of just men; the third layer of thirty-five stones consists of prophets and ministers of the Lord; the forty stones, which form the uppermost part of the tower-wall, consist of apostles and teachers who preach the Son of God.

Dronke suggests that Patrick uses the Hermas parable, which would have been almost as familiar to his Latin readership as the New Testament itself, to describe his own history. However unworthy and ill-equipped he may have been, he now belongs to that fourth uppermost group in the wall of the tower: he is one of the *'apostoli et doctores'*. Dronke concludes: 'the symbol is integral to his dialectic of self-accusation and self-defence.'

13   *Quis me stultum excitavit de medio eorum qui videntur sapientes.* This is a good example of the numerous phrases which show the influence of St Paul on Patrick. The Vulgate of 1 Cor 1: 27 reads: *Quae stulta sunt mundi elegit Deus ut confundat sapientes?*

D. S. Nerney's 'Study of St Patrick's Sources'[8] is still the most comprehensive analysis of the Pauline influence on Patrick. He demonstrates conclusively that Patrick often follows Paul not only in the spirit but in the style and even the idiom of the letters to the Corinthians. Compare, for example, Paul's *nihil sum* (2 Cor 12:11) with Patrick's *nihil valeo nisi ipse mihi dederit* (C 57) or *nam etsi imperitus sermone* (2 Cor 11: 6) with *pertimeo denudare imperitiam meam* (C 10) or *non in sapientia verbi* (1 Cor 1:17) with *inscientia mea, tardior linqua* (C 11).

Human inadequacy as a means of revealing God's power is only one of a series of arguments used by Patrick to justify his mission and vindicate himself against the *seniores*. The arguments are similar to Paul's defence of his mission in his second letter to the Corinthians where a faction set out to discredit him. Both mention: (1) the physical sufferings, labours and risk to life; for example, Paul mentions eight perils (2 Cor 11:26), Patrick twelve (C 35); (2) the establishment of a large and flourishing Christian community (2 Cor 10:13-15; C 38); (3) total disinterestedness in the service of God, for example, in the use of money (2 Cor 8:20-21, C 49-50); (4) their sincerity of conscience and devotion to truth (2 Cor 1:12, C 48); (5) an appeal to God as witness (2 Cor 1:23, 2 Cor 11:31, C 31, C 44).

16 I have taken *spiritus* here in both cases to refer to Patrick's human spirit rather than the Holy Spirit.

17 This section begins the sequence of dreams in the Confession which Patrick uses to chart the growing intensity of his relationship with God and to explain the personal discernment which led him step by step into his vocation as a missionary in Ireland and his ultimate commitment of himself to his mission to the exclusion of all else. In all there were seven dreams; three describe voices only (C 17, 21, 24), three describe voices and visions (C 23, 25, 29), and one a terrifying nightmare (C 20).

Each of the dreams (or pair of dreams as in 17) has its own distinct context and is carefully chosen to highlight a particular stage on Patrick's journey of faith.

C 17 occurs towards the end of his period of slavery in Ireland where he had gradually built up a life of continuous prayer for himself. Patrick was receptive to the dream because of his vivid awareness of God's closeness even though the content of the message was unexpected and laden with high risk. Runaway slaves were shown no mercy.

C 20 describes a shattering nightmare that haunted Patrick for the rest of his life. He saw it as a crushing encounter with Satan which followed his rejection of pagan ritual. He mentions two occasions when he was under moral although not physical pressure to conform to the paganism of his companions in whose power he found himself. Far from being inclined to make concessions, he saw himself as reaching out to them with his own supremely confident Christian faith. The price he paid was an experience of the intense and ominous oppressiveness of a morbid and debilitating atmosphere, like the scene of the witches in Shakespeare's *Macbeth*. It was as if the superstitious and brooding fears of his fellow-travellers were finally catching up with him. The nightmare took the form of a huge rock bearing down on top of him, leaving him paralysed and threatening total destruction. The ensuing panic and frantic terror he recognised as the force of Satan, the power of enveloping and suffocating evil in the confused darkness of the night. His recovery was a tangled combination of three factors of which he was only partly conscious at the time but recalled vividly at the time of writing; the hysterical and tortured plea to the prophet Elias, the brilliance of the morning sun and the calming, sustaining power of Christ. For note on Elias see C 20 below.

C 23 tells the best-known of all Patrick's dreams, the call of the Irish for him to walk once more among them. This was the dream that made Patrick decide to return to Ireland. Noel Dermot O'Donoghue[9] makes the point that the voices in the dream did not ask for preaching or baptism but only that Patrick as one specially endowed *(sancte puer)* should come back and share their lives. This endorses the modern view that there were many Christians already in Ireland during the period of Patrick's captivity (see chapter two, Commentary, pp. 39, 47, 52). The point is important also because it gives the real-life context to which the vision relates. For notes on the content of this dream see C 23 below.

The next two dreams (C 24 and C 25) are linked by similar expressions of divine indwelling *(qui loquitur in te,* C 24, and *qui in me orabat,* C 25). In C 24 the person praying in him is identified as Christ; in C 25 he is the Holy Spirit. The distinction shows that Patrick's relationship with the Trinity was much more than the intellectual acceptance of a credal formula, that his consciousness was so filled with the unity of the Trinity and the different associations and functions of the three distinct persons that the awareness carried over into sleep and dreams. To put it simply, Patrick met each of the three persons of the Trinity and became absorbed in all three.

The final vision (C 29), even more than any of the others, has a special sense of immediacy with its context. Patrick had been condemned in a formal document delivered by his enemies. That night in his dream he saw the document again and simultaneously he heard God's voice not merely clearing his good name but identifying with him personally. The effect was to restore his morale and to give him the conviction and energy to vindicate himself in the eyes of his critics, which he duly did. This condemnation and subsequent vindication are the climax of the entire Confession and were the basic reason for its composition. They also bring the sequence of dream stories to a conclusion.

17 *ducenta milia passus* means literally two hundred thousand paces or two hundred Roman miles. The equivalent in statute measure is about a hundred and eighty miles.

17-22 Patrick's encounter with the pagan sailors is by far the most sustained narrative of the Confession. Apart from giving the context of the nightmare experience already mentioned (see explanatory note on dreams, pp. 75-6), the passage is an interesting cameo of two ways of life which had basic human needs in common but differed in every other way. The sailors held the initiative; they agreed to take Patrick on board but only when they had persuaded the captain to do so; they tried to force him to conform to specifically pagan practices (sucking the nipples and sacrificing wild honey) which were repugnant to Patrick; he was an isolated prisoner among them for sixty days. Patrick impressed them with his Christian God at the cost of a bruising encounter with Satan.

20 The linking of the sun with the prophet Elijah and Christ reflects in retrospect Patrick's later efforts to convert the Irish from sun-worship which he mentions explicitly in C 60. Ludwig Bieler is worth quoting on this strange experience and the fusion in Patrick's mind of the prophet Elijah and the sun-god Helios:

> This fusion was common in ancient Christian art and literature. It has two causes: the similarity of their Greek form-names *(Helias - Helios)*, and the reminiscences of the sun-god in his

chariot that were evoked by the fiery chariot in which the prophet was taken to heaven (2 Kings 2:11). There may have been at the back of Patrick's mind some dim recollection of a picture or mosaic representing the assumption of Elias [Elijah] after the traditional representations of Helios driving through the sky.

The sun that dispelled Patrick's nightmare was, of course, understood by him as the *sol verus* (the messianic *sol iustitiae*, Mal 4:2), Christ. Here again we have the very interesting parallelism of a Christian tradition conceiving of Christ, the creator of the sun, as the sun of our salvation *(sol salutis)* opposed to the pagan and imperial sun-god *(sol invictus)*. Christ as the true sun and God of resurrection and salvation was also represented in art as ascending in a fiery chariot; see now the most interesting mosaic discovered in the recent excavations in St Peter's, Rome. The mosaic was found on the vault of a mausoleum which was originally pagan, but radically transformed into a Christian place of burial.[10]

23 The content of this vision has often been compared with St Paul's call to Macedonia in Acts 16:9-10: *Et visio per noctem Paulo ostensa est, vir Macedo quasi stans et deprecans eum, dicens: transiens in Macedoniam, adjuva nos* (A vision was shown to Paul by night, a Macedonian man as if standing and imploring him: cross over into Macedonia, help us).

Victoricus: The reading of the manuscripts accepted by Howlett (see note under C 9 above) is Victoricius. This is closer to Victricius, a well-known bishop of Rouen at the beginning of the fifth century, who would have been an ideal model for a young man from Britain or Gaul aspiring to be a missionary among rural people.

Vox Hiberionacum: This is one of two names Patrick uses to describe his Irish converts, see also *ad hibernas gentes* (C 37) and *hiberionaci* (L 16). The other is *filii scottorum* (C 41, L 12), *una scotta* (C 42).

The distinction seems to refer to rank, the *hiberionaci* to commoners, the *scotti* to nobility. *Scotti* is also used of those who plundered Patrick's mission but always along with the Picts (L 2, 12). As the Picts lived in what is now Scotland, it looks as if the *Scotti* – but only those *Scotti* who were in league with them as fellow-plunderers of Patrick's mission – were migrants or descendants of migrants from Ireland to Scotland.

32 For *defensio* as 'interdiction, prohibition', I have consulted the dictionaries of Blaise and Chirat, Niermeyer, and Latham and Howlett.[11]

The negative meaning of *defensio* here is demanded by the context of the entire incident (C 26-32) and is roughly synonymous with *reprobatus sum* (C 29). Patrick was put on trial and his accusers came to inform him of the result which was an outright rejection of his episcopal mission. The rejection took the form of a written censure or interdict which deprived Patrick of his good name (*quod scriptum erat contra faciem meam sine honore* C 29). The possibility that it went as far as declaring him deposed may seem initially to be overstretching the evidence but cannot be ruled out, given the intense and prolonged animosity against him, the extreme degree of personal hurt he describes (*conculcatio*, C 26, literally, trampling down) and the lengths to which he goes to prove his total innocence of the charges against him. There is clearly much more than injured vanity here.

Jean Gaudemet leaves us in no doubt as to the potential seriousness of the main charge against Patrick in the canon law of the period. He also discusses the many references to depositions and attempted depositions of bishops and observes that the law was not as precise as it later became.[12]

42 Beginning with the *benedicta scotta* at the top of the social ladder, Patrick lists the four categories of holy women whom he had introduced to a life of a consecrated virginity. These are: (1) those who suffer for their commitment at the hands of their own pagan

families, (2) those born in Ireland of the same race as Patrick (i.e. British), (3) widows and those who have foregone their marriage rights (*continentes*), (4) those held in slavery.

The first category were Patrick's own converts. He marvels at their courage under intense domestic pressure and records that their numbers are increasing, presumably from the low base one would expect in view of all the opposition. When he comes to describe the second category, the contrast is sharp and striking. Patrick is more matter of fact. There is no mention of persecution or undue hardship, merely that the virgins are beyond counting, an indication that they came from Christian homes and that they were spread over a wide area. Because he takes the credit for it, we can be sure that it was Patrick who introduced tham to the consecrated life, but they needed much less attention and protection than his converts. Their families would appear to have been British Christians who had settled in Ireland, perhaps initially through slavery, and who made a substantial contribution to the spread of Christianity in Ireland and the growth of monasticism. That Patrick mentions them means that he was in touch with at least one group of Christians in Ireland other than his own converts.

Patrick has no illusion about the difficulties of the female slaves who were at the bottom of society at the time and for many years to come. The sixth-century *Penitential of Finnian*, for example, attempted to legislate against the use of slave women for sexual purposes. Nevertheless, the law-text *Córus Béscnai* quoted a prophecy about Patrick that 'he will free slaves, he will elevate the low-born'.[13]

The verb at the end of this section, *imitantur*, has no object, unlike the other examples of the same verb in C 47 and C 59. In meaning, however, if not in syntax, it relates easily to *Dominus* in the previous line. For Patrick, God himself is the source of the consecrated life. It is he alone who gives the grace of virginity. Those to whom he gives it have always been seen by the Fathers of the Christian Church as images of the eternal and all-holy God. In the memorable words of one of them, Gregory of Nyssa, 'Christianity is the imitation of the divine nature'.[14]

50 A *scriptula* or *scrupulum* was a small silver coin, one twenty-fourth part of an ounce.

53 Patrick obviously did not enjoy the right to travel freely which the learned classes had and which churchmen later obtained. He would have had, however, among his converts men with the legal standing that enabled them to participate in the treaties and agreements between one *tuath* and another. This legal standing was based on an honour-price which was the measure of a man's status in society and, among other things, his right to go surety. By paying the honour-price to the brehons Patrick was buying the right to travel to different *tuatha* as often as he pleased, with all the legal guarantees due to the man whose honour-price it was. This honour-price seems to be what Patrick means by *pretium*.[15]

60 Patrick is explicit about his rejection of sun-worship; 'those who worship it will be severely punished.' Sun-worship was evidently widely practised among the Celts; but it was also a feature of the Teutonic peoples who have left us the word Sunday for the first day of the week and of the Roman Empire. See note on C 20 above.

61-2 Even though Patrick uses the verb *confiteri* four times in the first five sections, only at the end does the key word *confessio* occur. *Confessio* is a specific literary genre with its own place in the tradition of the Latin Church and has to be interpreted as such. The recognised masterpiece of the genre belongs to the great Augustine of Hippo who provided the definitive model of Confessions for those who came after him. It is in this general sense rather than searching for direct quotations or idiomatic patterns that it is legitimate to make connections between the work of Patrick and his illustrious predecessor.[16]

LETTER TO THE SOLDIERS
OF COROTICUS

1 Patrick's proclamation of himself here as bishop contrasts with the opening of the Confession and highlights the basic difference between the two writings. The Confession is a statement of personal faith whereas the Letter is a decree of excommunication, drawn up with all the legal authority that Patrick could muster. On closer examination, however, Patrick's credentials as a bishop are also of crucial importance in the structure of the Confession. Howlett in his recent study identifies the phrase at the precise centre of his word count (C 26): *Ecce dandus es tu ad gradum episcopatus*.[1]

2 Patrick distinguishes four groups: (1) Coroticus, and his soldiers, (2) Picts, (3) Scoto-Irish and (4) apostates.

Coroticus and his soldiers were nominal Christians, which explains why he wrote to them at all and in such anger. Given his proximity to the Picts, who certainly belonged to what is now Scotland, it is most likely that scholars have correctly identified Coroticus as the Coirthech described in a chapter-heading of Muirchú's *Vita Sancti Patricii* in the *Book of Armagh*: *de conflictu sancti Patricii adversum Coirthech regem Aloo*. Aloo is taken to be *Ail Cluaide*, the Strathclyde citadel at Dumbarton Rock.[2]

The name *Picti*, literally, 'the painted ones', was given by the Romans to a group of tribes who lived north of the Clyde-Forth isthmus. Charles Thomas, who has studied the archaeological and place-name evidence, traces their incursions southwards and into the Lowlands from the end of the fourth century. This would have brought them into close contact, more often as rivals than as neighbours, with other post-Roman British peoples, among them the subjects of our Coroticus.

Their partners in the slave-trading business, the *Scotti*, were originally seafarers from Ireland and of the same race as the Irish nobility of the same name so highly praised by Patrick both here (L 12) and in the Confession (C 41, 42). They gradually settled along the west coast of Scotland, mainly in Argyll, and in the sixth century were evangelised by Colmcille's monks from Iona.[3]

The apostates are undefined racially but from a second reference in L 15 it is clear that, as renegade Christians and along with the murderous soldiers of Coroticus, they share the full force of Patrick's fury.

This tentative historical and geographical construction would suggest strongly that the attack on Patrick's neophytes took place somewhere near the north-east Irish coast. Patrick was at the scene himself (L 12), he was in Ireland, an exile from his own country (L 10), the attack came from Britain where Patrick's 'own people' lived (L 11), he was able to identify the source of the attack and register his protest immediately (L 2-3), he was well briefed on the contacts between Coroticus and the border areas of northern Britain where the *Scotti* and the Picts carried on their slave trade (L 2).

3 The communal initiation liturgy outlined here is of special interest in tracing the historical development of the rite of confirmation. The significant details are: (1) the linking of baptism with confirmation in what seems to have been a single ceremony, (2) the anointing with chrism on the forehead, (3) the performance of the entire rite by Patrick himself. This tallies exactly with the structure described in detail in the *Apostolic Tradition* of Hippolytus in the early third century. Hippolytus, however, does not indicate the special giving of the Holy Spirit that we associate with confirmation today, rather a post-baptismal anointing centred on the messianic role of Christ, which of course included the Holy Spirit but in a less distinctive way. In the light of this it is to be noted that Patrick speaks of confirming in Christ *(in Christo confirmavi)* at the end of section 2 of the Letter and that nowhere does he mention a laying on of hands with invocation of the Holy Spirit. (One must add immediately that any information he

gives on ritual is incidental and is not germane to his subject.) On the other hand Patrick's reference to the anointing on the forehead *(in fronte)* is in line with a letter of Pope Innocent I around 416 associating anointing on the forehead exclusively with the bishop. Presbyters may anoint on the head at the post-baptismal chrismation, bishops alone anoint on the forehead. Innocent's second innovation was to give the Holy Spirit a clear and distinctive role but, as we have seen, there is no hint of this shift of emphasis in Patrick's account.[4]

5   Patrick uses *alieni* here, stopping short of the technical term *excommunicati;* but excommunication is clearly what is meant. Patrick uses his full authority as a properly constituted bishop of the Christian Church to declare Coroticus and his soldiers to be cut off formally from the community of the Church. He imposes the penalty of excommunication in the same style as the decree of Pope Innocent I (401-17), no doubt in order to give extra effect to his letter.

The full import of the excommunication is spelled out in detail by Patrick in section 7. To dine with sinners was forbidden on the authority of St Paul, 1 Cor 5:11. Those excommunicated had to 'make reparation to God through rigorous penance', a reminder that in those days before the separation of the internal forum of conscience and the external forum of canon law and when all penance was public, it would have been difficult to distinguish between those who were excommunicated and those who admitted serious sin and were thereby publicly obliged to do penance. A further question for Church historians is how Patrick felt entitled to demand that his letter should be read not only directly to Coroticus himself but *coram cunctis plebibus* which I have taken to mean local communities of Christians (L 21). This may mean that the local bishop of Coroticus was bypassed which even in the fifth century would hardly have been approved. On the other hand, the reference to *sacerdotes* (L 6) – which we have seen in note C 11 above can mean bishops – may imply that Patrick had the passive if not the active backing of the local bishop for his drastic *démarche*.

10 That Patrick's father was a decurion meant that he held public office in a town organised on the Roman pattern. This is one of the arguments, supported by archaeological evidence, in favour of locating Patrick's home region in the Severn Valley or the West Country where the structures of Roman urban administration had a longer life than in any other area in Britain.

18 According to Bieler, *cum apostolis et prophetis atque martyribus* recalls the well-known Latin hymn, the *Te Deum*, which survived mainly through Irish manuscripts like the Antiphonary of Bangor. Bieler finds another trace of the same hymn in C 4 where *quem credimus* occurs unexpectedly in the middle of the creed.[5] Another straw in the same wind is the title of the hymn *Te Deum laudamus* which occurs for the first time in the Rule of St Caesarius for monks, written probably before 502 when he was Abbot of Lerins. Could Lerins be where Patrick picked it up?[6]

21 I have used Finan's translation of *coram cunctis plebibus* as 'before all the communities'[7] in order to convey that Patrick's letter was canonical and church-related rather than a secular document.

NOTES

CONFESSION
1. Albert Blaise and Henri Chirat, *Dictionnaire Latin-Francais des auteurs Chrétiens* (Strasbourg, 1954), p. 751.
2. Gerhart B. Ladner, *The Idea of Reform: Its Impact on Christian Thought and Action in the Age of the Fathers* (Cambridge, Mass: Harvard University Press, 1959), pp. 343-8.
3. Michael Herren, 'Mission and Monasticism in the *Confessio* of Patrick', in *Sages, Saints and Storytellers: Celtic Studies in Honour of Professor James Carney*, ed. Donnchadh Ó Corráin, Liam Breathnach and Kim McCone (Maynooth, 1989), pp. 76-85.

4.   Peter Dronke, 'St Patrick's Reading', *Cambridge Medieval Studies,* no. 1 (summer 1981), pp. 21-38.
5.   D. R. Howlett, *The Book of Letters of Saint Patrick the Bishop* (Dublin: Four Courts Press, 1994).
6.   Colmán Etchingham, preface to *Who Was Saint Patrick?*, by E. A. Thompson (1985; reprint with preface, Woodbridge, 1999), pp. xxii-xxvi.
7.   Peter Dronke (as cited in 3 above), pp. 37-8.
8.   D. S. Nerney, 'A Study of St Patrick's Sources', in *Irish Ecclesiastical Record,* vol. 72 (1949), pp. 497-507, vol. 73 (1950), pp. 14-26, 97-110, 265-280.
9.   Noel Dermot O'Donoghue, *Aristocracy of Soul: Patrick of Ireland* (London, 1987), p. 20.
10. Ludwig Bieler, *The Works of St Patrick, St Secundinus Hymn on St Patrick* (London: Westminster Maryland, 1953), p. 84.
11. Blaise and Chirat (as cited in 1 above), p. 246; Niermeyer, *Mediae Latinitatis Lexicon Minus, Lexique Latin Médieval-Francais/Anglais* (Leiden, 1954), p. 312; and especially Lathan and Howlett, *Dictionary of Medieval Latin from British Sources,* vol. 1, D-E (British Academy, Oxford University Press, 1986), pp. 587-9.
12. Jean Gaudemet, *L'Église dans l'Empire Romain IVe-Ve siècles* (Paris: Sirey, 1958), pp. 365-6.
13. Fergus Kelly, *A Guide to Early Irish Law* (Dublin, 1998), p. 96.
14. Gerhart B. Ladner, (as cited in 2 above), p. 91.
15. This note is based on Kelly (as cited in 12 above), especially pp. 4-5, 8-9.
16. See Thomas Finan, 'The Literary Genre of St Patrick's Pastoral Letters', in *The Letters of Saint Patrick,* Daniel Conneely (Maynooth: An Sagart, 1993), pp. 131-50, who develops the thinking of Dronke (as cited in 3 above).

LETTER TO THE SOLDIERS OF COROTICUS
1.   D. R. Howlett, *The Book of Letters of Saint Patrick the Bishop* (Dublin: Four Courts Press, 1994).

2.   David Dumville, *Saint Patrick AD 493-1993* (Woodbridge, 1993), pp. 107-115.

3.   See Charles Thomas, *Christianity in Roman Britain to AD 500* (London, 1981), pp. 285-8.

4.   This note is based on Aidan Kavanagh, *Confirmation: Origins and Reform* (New York, 1988), especially pp. 41-71.

5.   See Ludwig Bieler, *Libri Epistolarum Sancti Patricii Episcopi Part 2* (Dublin, 1952), pp. 207, 105 and *The Works of St Patrick, St Secundinus Hymn on St Patrick* (London: Westminster Maryland, 1953), p. 93.

6.   *The Catholic Encyclopedia* (New York, 1912), vol. 14, p. 468.

7.   Daniel Conneely, *The Letters of Saint Patrick* (Maynooth: An Sagart, 1993), p. 81.

APPENDICES

CONFESSIO / AN FHAOISTIN

Repaying a debt

¹ I am Patrick, a sinner, the most rustic and least of all the faithful, the most contemptible in the eyes of a great many people. My father was Calpornius, a deacon and the son of the presbyter Potitus. He came from the village of Bannaventaberniae where he had a country residence nearby. It was there that I was taken captive.

I was almost sixteen at the time and I did not know the true God. I was taken into captivity to Ireland with many thousands of people. We deserved this fate because we had turned away from God; we neither kept his commandments nor obeyed our priests who used to warn us about our salvation. The Lord's fury bore down on us and he scattered us among many heathen peoples, even to the ends of the earth. This is where I now am, in all my insignificance, among strangers.

² The Lord there made me aware of my unbelief that I might at last advert to my sins and turn whole-heartedly to the Lord my God. He showed concern for my weakness, and pity for my youth and ignorance; he watched over me before I got to know him and before I was wise or distinguished good from evil. In fact he protected me and comforted me as a father would his son. ³ I cannot be silent then, nor indeed should I, about the great benefits and grace which the Lord saw fit to confer on me in the land of my captivity. This is the way we repay God for correcting us and taking notice of us; we honour and praise his wonders before every nation under heaven.

1 Ego Patricius peccator rusticissimus et minimus omnium fidelium et contemptibilissimus apud plurimos patrem habui Calpornium diaconum filium quendam Potiti presbyteri, qui fuit uico Bannauenta Berniae; uillulam enim prope habuit, ubi ego capturam dedi. Annorum eram tunc fere sedecim. Deum enim uerum ignorabam et Hiberione in captiuitate adductus sum cum tot milia hominum secundum merita nostra, quia 'a Deo recessimus', et 'praecepta eius non custodiuimus' et sacerdotibus nostris non oboedientes fuimus, qui nostram salutem admonebant, et Deus 'induxit super nos iram animationis suae et dispersit nos in gentibus' multis etiam 'usque ad ultimum terrae', ubi nunc paruitas mea esse uidetur inter alienigenas, 2 et ibi 'Dominus aperuit sensum incredulitatis meae' ut uel sero rememorarem delicta mea et ut 'conuerterem toto corde ad Dominum Deum meum', qui 'respexit humilitatem meam' et misertus est adolescentiae et ignorantiae meae et custodiuit me antequam scirem eum et antequam saperem uel distinguerem inter bonum et malum et muniuit me et consolatus est me ut pater filium.

3 Unde autem tacere non possum 'neque expedit quidem' tanta beneficia et tantam gratiam quam mihi Dominus praestare dignatus est 'in terra captiuitatis meae', quia haec est retributio nostra, ut post correptionem uel agnitionem Dei 'exaltare et confiteri mirabilia eius coram omni natione quae est sub omni caelo.'

1 Mise Pádraig, peacach róthútach agus is lú tábhacht de na fíréin go léir, an té is mó a bhfuil dímheas air i measc mórán daoine. Ba é Calpornius m'athair, deagánach agus mac don chruifear Potitus. Ba as sráidbhaile Bannaventaberniae é agus bhí teach cónaithe aige faoin tuath i ngar dó. Ba ansin a gabhadh mé. Bhí mé chóir a bheith sé bliana déag ag an am agus ní raibh aithne agam ar an fhíor-Dhia. Tugadh mé mar chime go hÉirinn i gcuideachta na mílte duine eile. Bhí sé seo tuillte againn mar gur thréigeamar Dia; níor choinníomar a chuid aitheanta nó ní rabhamar umhal dár sagairt a bhíodh ag tabhairt comhairle ár slánaithe dúinn. Lig an Tiarna a racht amach orainn agus scaip sé muid i measc mórán págánach fiú go dtí críocha na cruinne. Seo an áit a bhfuil mé le feiceáil anois go suarach i measc na gcoimhthíoch.

2 Chuir an Tiarna ar an eolas mé faoi m'easnamh creidimh i nDia ag súil go smaointeoinn ar mo pheacaí agus dóchas ó mo chroí a chur sa Tiarna mo Dhia. Bhí imní air faoi mo laige agus bhí trua aige dom as siocair m'óige agus m'aineolais; choinnigh sé súil orm sula bhfuair mé aithne air agus sula raibh mé céillí go leor le haithne idir an mhaith agus an t-olc. Le fírinne, chosain sé mé agus thug sé faoiseamh dom mar a bhéarfadh athair dá mhac.

3 Ní thig liom, mar sin, nó níor chóir dom, a bheith i mo thost faoi na suáilcí agus na grástaí a shocair an Tiarna a bhronnadh orm ins an tír a raibh mé i ngéibheann ann. Seo an dóigh a dtugaimid aitheantas do Dhia as suim a chur ionainn agus muid a chur ar bhealach ár leasa; tugaimid onóir agus moladh dá thíolacthaí os comhair gach náisiún faoi gach spéir.

Profession of faith in the Trinity

4 There is no other God,
there never was and there never will be,
than God the Father
unbegotten and without beginning,
from whom is all beginning,
holding all things as we have learned;
and his son Jesus Christ
whom we declare
to have been always with the Father
and to have been begotten spiritually by the Father
in a way which baffles description,
before the beginning of the world,
before all beginning;
and through him are made all things, visible and invisible.

⁴ Quia non est alius Deus
nec umquam fuit ante nec erit post haec
praeter Deum Patrem ingenitum, sine principio,
a quo est omne principium,
omnia tenentem, ut didicimus,
et huius filium Iesum Xpistum,
quem cum Patre scilicet
semper fuisse testamur,
ante originem saeculi spiritaliter apud Patrem inenarrabiliter genitum
ante omne principium,
et per ipsum facta sunt uisibilia et inuisibilia,

⁴ Níl Dia ar bith eile ann,
ní raibh riamh agus ní bheidh a choíche,
ach amháin Dia ár nAthair
gan ghiniúint gan tús,
ar uaidh gach tús,
ar leis gach ní mar a d'fhoghlamaíomar;
agus a mhac Íosa Críost
a dhearbhaímid
a bhí i gcónaí leis an Athair
agus a gineadh ón Athair go spioradálta
ar dhóigh dho-inste
ó thús an domhain,
roimh an uile thosach;
agus is tríd a dhéantar gach ní, infheicthe agus dofheicthe.

He was made man,
defeated death
and was received into heaven by the Father,
who has given him all power over all names
in heaven, on earth, and under the earth;
and every tongue should acknowledge to him
that Jesus Christ is the Lord God.
We believe in him
and we look for his coming soon
as judge of the living and of the dead,
who will treat every man according to his deeds.
He has poured out the Holy Spirit on us in abundance,
the gift and guarantee of eternal life,
who makes those who believe and obey
sons of God and joint heirs with Christ.
We acknowledge and adore him
as one God in the Trinity of the holy name.

hominem factum,
morte deuicta in caelis ad Patrem receptum,
'et dedit illi omnem potestatem super omne nomen
caelestium et terrestrium et infernorum
et omnis lingua confiteatur ei
quia Dominus et Deus est Iesus Xpistus',
quem credimus et expectamus adventum ipsius mox futurum,
'iudex uiuorum atque mortuorum,
qui reddet unicuique secundum facta sua':
et 'effudit in nobis abunde Spiritum Sanctum,
donum' et 'pignus' immortalitatis,
qui facit credentes et oboedientes
ut sint 'filii Dei' et 'coheredes Xpisti',
quem confitemur et adoramus
unum Deum in Trinitate sacri nominis.

Rinneadh duine de,
sháraigh sé an bás
agus thug an tAthair isteach ins na flaithis é,
thug sé dó achan chumhacht os cionn gach uile ainm
ar neamh, ar talamh, agus faoin talamh;
agus admhaíodh gach duine dó
gurb é Íosa Críost an Tiarna Dia.
Creidimid ann
agus táimid ag súil lena theacht gan mhoill
mar bhreitheamh ar bheo agus ar mhairbh,
le cúiteamh a thabhairt de réir a ngníomhartha.
Dháil sé an Spiorad Naomh go fairsing orainn,
bronntanas agus geall na beatha síoraí,
a dhéanann clannmhac Dé agus comhoidhrí le Críost
díobh siúd a chreideann agus atá umhal dó.
Dearbhaímid agus adhraímid é
mar an t-aon Dia amháin i dTríonóid an ainm naofa.

Reasons for writing

5 He himself has said through the prophet: *Call upon me in the day of your trouble; and I will deliver you, and you shall glorify me.* He also says: *It is honourable to reveal and confess the works of God.* 6 Although I am imperfect in many ways I want my brothers and relatives to know what kind of man I am, so that they may perceive the aspiration of my life. 7 I know well the statement of the Lord which he makes in the psalm: *You will destroy those who speak falsely.* He says again: *A lying mouth destroys the soul.* The same Lord says in the Gospel: *On the day of judgement men will render account for every careless word they utter.* 8 I ought therefore to dread with fear and trembling the sentence of that day when no one will be able to escape or hide, but when all of us will have to give an account of even our smallest sins before the court of the Lord Christ.

9 For this reason I long had a mind to write, but held back until now. I was afraid of drawing general gossip on myself because I had not studied like the others who thoroughly imbibed the law and theology, both in equal measure. They never had to change their medium of speech since childhood but were able rather to improve their mastery of it while I, on the other hand, had to express myself in a foreign language. Anyone can easily see from the flavour of my writing how little training and skill in the use of words I got. As Scripture says: *Through the way he expresses himself shall the wise man be discerned, and his understanding and knowledge and instruction in truth.*

10 But what good is an excuse, no matter how genuine, especially since I now presume to take up in my old age what I failed to do as a young man? It was my sins then which prevented me from making my own of what I had read superficially. But who believes me although I should repeat what I said at the beginning?

⁵ Ipse enim dixit per prophetam 'Inuoca me in die tribulationis tuae et liberabo te et magnificabis me.' Et iterum inquit 'Opera autem Dei reuelare et confiteri honorificum est.' ⁶ Tamen etsi in multis imperfectus sum opto 'fratribus et cognatis' meis scire qualitatem meam, ut possint perspicere uotum animae meae. ⁷ Non ignoro 'testimonium Domini mei', qui in psalmo testatur 'Perdes eos qui loquuntur mendacium'. Et iterum inquit 'Os quod mentitur occidit animam'. Et idem Dominus in euangelio inquit, 'Uerbum otiosum quod locuti fuerint homines reddent pro eo rationem in die iudicii'. ⁸ Unde autem uehementer debueram 'cum timore et tremore' metuere hanc sententiam in die illa ubi nemo se poterit subtrahere uel abscondere, sed omnes omnino 'reddituri sumus rationem' etiam minimorum peccatorum 'ante tribunal Domini Xpisti'.

⁹ Quapropter olim cogitaui scribere, sed et 'usque nunc' haesitaui; timui enim ne 'inciderem in linguam' hominum, quia non didici 'sicut' et 'ceteri', qui optime itaque iura et sacras litteras utraque pari modo combiberunt et sermones illorum ex infantia numquam mutarunt, sed magis 'ad perfectum' semper addiderunt. Nam 'sermo et loquela' nostra translata est in linguam alienam, sicut facile potest probari ex saliua scripturae meae qualiter 'sum ego' in sermonibus instructus atque 'eruditus', quia, inquit, 'Sapiens per linguam dinoscetur et sensus et scientia et doctrina ueritatis'. ¹⁰ Sed quid prodest excusatio 'iuxta ueritatem', praesertim cum praesumptione, quatenus modo ipse adpeto 'in senectute' mea quod 'in iuuentute' non comparaui, quod obstiterunt peccata mea ut confirmarem quod ante perlegeram. Sed quis me credit etsi dixero quod ante praefatus sum?

⁵ Óir dúirt sé féin trí ráiteas an fháidh: *Scairt orm ar lá na trioblóide; agus saorfaidh mé thú; agus bhéarfaidh tú urraim dom sa ghlóir.* Deir sé chomh maith: *Is rud uasal é saothar Dé a nochtú agus a dhearbhú.* ⁶ Cé go bhfuil mé lochtach ar mhórán dóigheanna ba mhaith liom fios a bheith ag mo bhráithre agus mo ghaolta cén sórt duine mé ionas go mbeidh tuigbheáil acu ar dhúil m'anama. ⁷ Tá a fhios agam go maith ráiteas an Tiarna sa salm: *Déanfaidh tú na daoine seo a insíonn an bhréag a scrios.* Deir sé arís: *Milleann an béal bréagach an t-anam.* Deir an Tiarna céanna sa Soiscéal: *Ar lá an bhreithiúnais bhéarfaidh siad cuntas ar gach focal fíll dár chan siad.* ⁸Ba chóir dom mar sin a bheith critheaglach, agus uamhan a bheith orm roimh an bhreithiúnas ar an lá sin, nach mbeidh aon duine ábalta éalú nó rudaí a cheilt ach go mbeidh orainn uilig cuntas a thabhairt fiú ar na peacaí is inmhaite os comhair chúirt an Tiarna Críost.
⁹ Ar an chúis seo bhí rún agam scríobh le fada ach choinnigh mé srian orm féin go dtí anois. Bhí eagla orm go mbeadh daoine go ginearálta ag cúlchaint orm as siocair nach ndearna mé staidéar dian mar a rinne na daoine eile ar an dlí agus ar an diagacht araon mar a chéile. Ní raibh orthu riamh an modh cainte a bhí acu ón chliabhán a athrú ach bhí siad ábalta a gcuid inniúlachta a fheabhsú nuair a bhí ormsa mé féin a chur i láthair i dteanga iasachta. Beidh sé soiléir d'aon duine ó bhlas mo chuid scríbhneoireachta a laghad oiliúna agus scil in úsáid focal a fuair mé. Mar a deir an Scrioptúr: *Is tríd an teanga a aithnítear an t-eagnaí, agus a thuigbheáil agus eolas agus teagasc san fhirinne.*
¹⁰ Ach cén tairbhe an leithscéal, dá fhírinní é, go mórmhór má tá dánaíocht ag dul leis, sa mhéid go bhfuil mé ag tnúth i mo sheanaois le rud ar theip orm a dhéanamh nuair a bhí mé óg. Ba iad mo pheacaí a choisc orm an rud a bhí léite go sciobtha agam a fhoghlaim i gceart. Ach cé a chreidfidh mé fiú má deirim arís an rud atá ráite agam cheana.

The letter may not be elegant

I was taken captive as an adolescent, almost a speechless boy, before I knew what to seek and what to avoid. This is why I blush with shame at this stage and positively quail at exposing my lack of learning. I am unable to open my heart and mind to those who are used to concise writing in a way that my words might express what I feel. [11] If, indeed, I had been equipped as others were, I would not be silent in making my reparation. And if by chance I seem to some to be pushing myself forward, with my lack of knowledge and my slow speech, it is after all written: *The tongues of stammerers will quickly learn to speak peace.* How much more, then, must we earnestly strive, we who are, in the words of Scripture, *a letter of Christ bearing salvation to the uttermost parts of the earth?* The letter may not be elegant but it is assuredly and most powerfully written on your hearts, not with ink but with the spirit of the living God. The Spirit elsewhere is a witness that even rustic ways have been created by the Most High.

God's gift must be told

[12] I am, then, first and foremost a rustic, an untaught refugee indeed who does not know how to provide for the future. But this much I know for sure. Before I was humbled I was like a stone lying in the deep mud. Then he who is mighty came and in his mercy he not only pulled me out but lifted me up and placed me at the very top of the wall. I must, therefore, speak publicly in order to repay the Lord for such wonderful gifts, gifts for the present and for eternity which the human mind cannot measure.

Adolescens, immo paene puer inuerbis, capturam dedi, antequam scirem quid adpetere uel quid uitare debueram. Unde ergo hodie erubesco et uehementer pertimeo denudare imperitiam meam, quia disertis breuitate 'sermone explicare' nequeo, sicut enim spiritus gestit et animus, et sensus monstrat adfectus. [11] Sed si itaque datum mihi fuisset 'sicut' et 'ceteris' uerumtamen non silerem 'propter retributionem'.

Et si forte uidetur apud aliquantos me in hoc praeponere cum mea inscientia et 'tardiori lingua', sed etiam scriptum est enim 'Linguae balbutientes uelociter discent loqui pacem'. Quanto magis nos adpetere debemus, qui sumus, inquit, 'epistola Xpisti in salutem usque ad ultimum terrae', et si non diserta sed rata et fortissima, 'scripta in cordibus uestris non atramento sed spiritu Dei uiui'. Et iterum Spiritus testatur 'Et rusticationem ab Altissimo creatam'.

[12] Unde ego primus rusticus profuga indoctus scilicet, 'qui nescio in posterum prouidere', sed illud 'scio certissime quia' utique 'priusquam humiliarer' ego eram uelut lapis qui iacet in 'luto profundo': et uenit 'qui potens est' et in 'sua misericordia' sustulit me et quidem scilicet sursum adleuauit et collocauit me in summo pariete, et inde fortiter debueram exclamare 'ad retribuendum' quoque aliquid 'Domino' pro tantis beneficiis eius hic et in aeternum, quae mens hominum aestimare non potest.

Gabhadh mé nuair nach raibh mé ach i mo ghlas-stócach, i mo pháiste ó thaobh cainte de, sula raibh a fhios agam caidé ba chóir dom a lorg nó a sheachaint. Seo an fáth a dtig lasadh i mo ghrua le náire agus go bhfuil eagla an domhain orm m'aineolas a nochtú. Ní thig liom mo smaointe a chur in iúl do dhaoine atá oilte i gcaint ghonta, sé sin, de réir mar is mian le mo spiorad agus m'aigne agus mar a léiríonn mo chuid mhothúcháin dom. [11] Dá mbronnfaí na tíolacthaí orm mar a bronnadh ar dhaoine eile ní i mo thost a bheinn ag lorg cúitimh. Agus má shíleann daoine áirithe go bhfuil mé mo bhrú féin chun tosaigh in ainneoin m'aineolais agus laige labhartha, tá sé scríofa fosta: *Ní bheidh stadairí i bhfad ag foghlaim chaint na síochána.* Caidé eile a chaithimid a dhéanamh go díograiseach, muidne atá i bhfocail an Scrioptúir: *inár litir ó Chríost ag tabhairt an tslánaithe go críocha na cruinne.* Más mí-ealaíonta féin an litir tá sé cinnte go bhfuil sí scríofa go daingean in bhur gcroí, ní le dúch ach le spiorad Dé bhí. In áit eile tugann an Spiorad fianaise: fiú an tútachas féin, is é an té is airde a chruthaigh é.

[12] Is tuatach mé go deimhin, dídeanaí gan foghlaim, nach fios dom soláthar don lá amárach. Ach bí cinnte de go bhfuil a fhios agam an méid seo. Sular tugadh céim síos dom bhí mé mar chloch ina luí go domhain sa chlábar. Ansin tháinig an té atá cumhachtach agus lena thrócaire ní hé amháin gur tharraing sé amach mé ach thóg sé suas mé go fíor-bharr an bhalla. Caithfidh mé, mar sin, labhairt go poiblí le haisíoc a thabhairt don Tiarna as na tíolacthaí a thug sé dom, tíolacthaí ar an saol seo agus ar feadh na síoraíochta nach féidir leis an aigne dhaonna a mheas.

[13] Let you be astonished, you great and small men who revere God! Let you, lords, clever men of letters, hear and examine this! Who was it who roused me, fool that I am, from among those who are considered wise, expert in law, powerful in speech and general affairs? He passed over these for me, a mere outcast. He inspired me with fear, reverence and patience to be the one who would if possible serve the people faithfully to whom the love of Christ brought me. The love of Christ indeed gave me to them to serve them humbly and sincerely for my entire lifetime if I am found worthy.

[14] My decision to write must be made, then, in the light of our faith in the Trinity. The gift of God and his eternal consolation must be made known, regardless of danger. I must fearlessly and confidently spread the name of God everywhere in order to leave a legacy after my death to my brothers and children, the many thousands of them, whom I have baptised in the Lord. [15] I am not at all worthy to receive so much grace after all the trials and difficulties, after captivity and so many years among that heathen people. The Lord, indeed, gave much to me, his little servant, more than as a young man I ever hoped for or even considered.

Daily prayer

When [16] I had come to Ireland I was tending herds every day and I used to pray many times during the day. More and more the love of God and reverence for him came to me. My faith increased and the spirit was stirred up so that in the course of a single day I would say as many as a hundred prayers, and almost as many in the night. This I did even when I was staying in the woods and on the mountain. Before dawn I used to be roused up to pray in snow or frost or rain. I never felt the worse for it; nor was I in any way lazy because, as I now realise, the spirit was burning within me.

13 Unde autem admiramini itaque 'magni et pusilli qui timetis Deum' et uos domini cati rethorici audite ergo et scrutamini quis me stultum excitauit de medio eorum qui uidentur esse sapientes et legis periti et 'potentes in sermone' et in omni re, et me quidem, detestabilis huius mundi, prae ceteris inspirauit si talis essem – dummodo autem – ut 'cum metu et reuerentia' et 'sine querella' fideliter prodessem genti ad quam 'caritas Xpisti' transtulit et donauit me in uita mea, si dignus fuero, denique ut cum humilitate et ueraciter deseruirem illis.

14 In 'mensura' itaque 'fidei' Trinitatis oportet distinguere sine reprehensione periculi notum facere 'donum Dei' et 'consolationem aeternam', sine timore fiducialiter Dei nomen ubique expandere, ut etiam 'post obitum meum' exagallias relinquere fratribus et filiis meis quos in Domino ego baptizaui tot milia hominum, 15 et non eram dignus neque talis ut hoc Dominus seruulo suo concederet, post aerumnas et tantas moles, post captiuitatem, post annos multos in gentem illam tantam gratiam mihi donaret, quod ego aliquando in iuuentute mea numquam speraui neque cogitaui.

16 Sed postquam Hiberione deueneram cotidie itaque pecora pascebam et frequens in die orabam, magis ac magis accedebat amor Dei et timor ipsius et fides augebatur et spiritus agebatur, ut in die una usque ad centum orationes et in nocte prope similiter, ut etiam in siluis et monte manebam, et ante lucem excitabar ad orationem per niuem, per gelu, per pluuiam, et nihil mali sentiebam neque ulla pigritia erat in me, sicut modo uideo, quia tunc spiritus in me feruebat,

13 Bíodh iontas oraibh mar sin, sibhse mór agus beag a bhfuil urraim agaibh do Dhia! Agus sibhse, tiarnaí agus ollúna foghlamtha, éistigí agus scrúdaígí seo. Cérbh é mar sin a spreag mise, an t-amadán, as lár an dreama a mheastar a bheith críonna oilte sa dlí, éifeachtach sa chaint agus i gcúrsaí an tsaoil? Rinne sé neamhiontas díobh ar mhaithe liomsa a bhfuil drochmheas air. Spreag sé mé le heagla, le hurraim agus le foighid ionas gur mise an duine – dá mb' fhéidir é – a bhéarfadh seirbhís dhílis do na daoine sin ar chuir Críost ina dtreo mé. Níl aon amhras ach gur thug grá Chríost le mo shaol mé dóibh, más fiú mé, chun seirbhís umhal ionraic a thabhairt dóibh.
14 Tá sé de dhualgas orm, mar sin, cinneadh a dhéanamh de réir mo chreidimh sa Tríonóid. Caithfear tíolacadh Dé agus a shólás síoraí a chraobhscaoileadh is cuma cén chontúirt a bhaineann leis. Caithfidh mé ainm Dé a chraoladh go dóchasach achan áit gan scáth gan eagla le hoidhreacht a fhágáil i ndiaidh mo bháis ag mo bhráithre agus a bpáistí, na mílte mílte acu a bhaist mé in ainm Dé. 15 Níl sé tuillte agam ar chor ar bith an oiread sin grásta a fháil i ndiaidh gach buaireamh agus deacracht, i ndiaidh géibhinn agus a bheith mórán blianta i measc págánach. Le fírinne thug an Tiarna go leor dom, a shearbhónta beag, níos mó mar fhear óg ná a raibh mé riamh ag súil leis nó fiú ar smaointigh mé air.
16 Nuair a tháinig mé go hÉirinn bhí mé ag buachailleacht tréada achan lá agus ba ghnáth liom urnaí go minic le linn an lae. Níos mó ná riamh mhéadaigh mo ghrá do Dhia agus m'umhlaíocht dó. Neartaigh mo chreideamh agus bhí an spiorad corraithe ionam sa dóigh go ndeirinn suas le céad paidir in imeacht lae agus chóir a bheith an méid céanna san oíche. Rinne mé é seo fiú nuair a bhínn ag fanacht ins na coillte agus ar an tsliabh. Roimh bhreacadh an lae mhúsclaítí mé le dhul ag urnaí sa sneachta, sa sioc agus sa bháisteach. Níor ghoill sé seo riamh orm nó ní raibh mé ar dhóigh ar bith falsa, nó mar a thuigim anois, bhí an spiorad ag borradh istigh ionam.

Taking flight

[17] In my sleep there indeed one night I heard a voice saying to me: 'It is well that you fast, soon you will go to your own country.' After a short while I again heard a voice saying: 'Look, your ship is ready.' It was quite a distance away, about two hundred miles; I never had been to the place, nor did I know anyone there. Shortly after that I ran away and left the man with whom I had spent six years. The power of God directed my way successfully and nothing daunted me until I reached that ship.

[18] The day I arrived the ship was set afloat and I spoke to the crew in order that I might be allowed to sail with them. But the captain was annoyed and he retorted angrily: 'On no account are you to try to go with us.' When I heard this I left them to go back to the little hut where I was lodging. On the way I began to pray, and before I had ended my prayer I heard one of them shouting loudly after me: 'Come quickly, these men are calling you.' I went back to them at once and they began to say to me: 'Come on, we will take you on trust; make your bond of friendship with us in any way you wish.' I refused on that day to suck their nipples out of reverence for God, but rather hoped they would come to faith in Jesus Christ for they were heathens. Thus I got my way with them and we set sail at once.

Food for the journey

[19] After three days we came to land and for twenty-eight days we made our way through deserted country. Supplies ran out and the party was the worse for hunger. One day the captain began to say to me: 'Tell me this, Christian. You say your God is great and all-powerful; why then can you not pray for us? As you see we are in danger of starving; it is unlikely indeed that we will ever see a human being again.' I said to them confidently: 'Turn sincerely with your whole heart to the Lord my God because nothing is impossible for him,

[17] et ibi scilicet quadam nocte in somno audiui uocem dicentem mihi 'Bene ieiunas cito iturus ad patriam tuam', et iterum post paululum tempus audiui 'responsum' dicentem mihi 'Ecce nauis tua parata est' et non erat prope, sed forte habebat ducenta milia passus et ibi numquam fueram nec ibi notum quemquam de hominibus habebam, et deinde postmodum conuersus sum in fugam et intermisi hominem cum quo fueram sex annis et ueni in uirtute Dei, qui uiam meam ad bonum dirigebat et nihil metuebam donec perueni ad nauem illam, [18] et illa die qua perueni profecta est nauis de loco suo, et locutus sum ut haberem unde nauigare cum illis et gubernator displicuit illi et acriter cum indignatione respondit 'Nequaquam tu nobiscum adpetes ire' et cum haec audiissem separaui me ab illis ut uenirem ad teguriolum ubi hospitabam, et in itinere coepi orare et antequam orationem consummarem audiui unum ex illis et fortiter exclamabat post me 'Ueni cito, quia uocant te homines isti', et statim ad illos reuersus sum, et coeperunt mihi dicere 'Ueni, quia ex fide recipimus te; fac nobiscum amicitiam quo modo uolueris' et in illa die itaque reppuli 'sugere mammellas eorum' propter timorem Dei, sed uerumtamen ab illis speraui uenire in fidem Iesu Xpisti, quia gentes erant, et ob hoc obtinui cum illis, et protinus nauigauimus.

[19] Et post triduum terram cepimus et uiginti octo dies per desertum iter fecimus et cibus defuit illis et 'fames inualuit super eos', et alio die coepit gubernator mihi dicere 'Quid est, Xpistiane? Tu dicis Deus tuus magnus et omnipotens est; quare ergo non potes pro nobis orare, quia nos a fame periclitamur; difficile est enim ut aliquem hominem umquam uideamus.' Ego enim confidenter dixi illis '"Convertemini" ex fide "ex toto corde ad Dominum Deum meum, quia nihil est impossibile illi"',

[17] Oíche amháin agus mé i mo chodladh chuala mé glór ag rá liom: 'Is maith an rud go mbíonn tú ag troscadh, ní bheidh sé i bhfad go mbeidh tú ag dul go dtí do thír féin.' I ndiaidh tamaill ghoirid chuala mé glór arís á rá: 'Amharc, tá do long réidh.' Bhí sé bealach fada ar shiúl, thart faoi dhá chéad míle; ní raibh mé riamh san áit nó ní raibh aithne agam ar aon duine ann. Tamall gearr ina dhiaidh sin d'éalaigh mé agus d'fhág mé an fear mé a raibh mé leis ar feadh sé bliana. Threoraigh cumhacht Dé ar bhealach mo leasa mé agus níor chuir a dhath eagla orm gur bhain mé an long amach.

[18] An lá a shroich mé an áit bhí an long réidh le dhul chun na farraige agus labhair mé leis an fhoireann le fáil amach an mbeadh cead agam seoladh leo. Ach ní raibh an caiptín sásta agus d'fhreagair sé go borb feargach: 'Níl maith ar bith duit a bheith ag iarraidh a dhul linne'. Nuair a chuala mé é seo d'fhág mé iad le dhul ar ais go dtí an bhothóg a raibh mé ag fanacht inti. Ar an bhealach thosaigh mé ag urnaí agus sula raibh an urnaí críochnaithe agam chuala mé duine acu ag scairteadh i mo dhiaidh os ard: 'Tar go gasta, tá na fir seo ag scairteadh ort.' Chuaigh mé ar ais láithreach agus thosaigh siad a rá liom: 'Tar anseo. Glacfaimid thú; cuir muinín ionainn agus déan cairdeas linn de réir mar is mian leat.' Dhiúltaigh mé an lá sin a gcíocha a dhiúl, de bharr umhlaíocht do Dhia, ach toisc gur phágánaigh iad bhí súil agam go dtiocfaidís chun creidimh in Íosa Críost. Is mar sin a d'éirigh liom ina gcuideachta agus chuireamar chun seoil láithreach bonn.

[19] I ndiaidh trí lá bhaineamar an talamh amach agus ar feadh ocht lá fichead rinneamar ár mbealach trí fhásach tíre. Bhí an soláthar bia rite agus bhí an t-ocras ag cur isteach ar an scaifte. Lá amháin thosaigh an caiptín a chaint liom mar seo: 'Inis seo dom, a Chríostaí. Deir tú go bhfuil Dia maith agus uilechumhachtach; cén fáth mar sin nach dtig leat guí ar ár son?' Mar a tchí tú táimid i gcontúirt bás a fháil den ocras; ní dócha go bhfeicfimid duine beo a choíche arís. 'Dúirt mé leo go muiníneach: 'Bígí dáiríre agus cuirigí bhur ndóchas ó chroí sa Tiarna mo Dhia, mar níl rud ar bith dodhéanta aige,

that this day he may send you food on your way until you are
satisfied; for he has plenty everywhere.' And with the help of God so
it happened. Suddenly a herd of pigs appeared on the road before our
eyes; they killed many of them and stopped there for two nights.

They were well fed, and had their fill of pork, for many of them had
grown weak and had been left half-dead along the way. After this they
gave profuse thanks to God and I became honourable in their eyes.
From that day they had plenty of food. They even found wild honey
and offered me some. One of them said; 'This is offered in sacrifice.'
Thank God, I tasted none of it.

Overcoming Satan

[20] The same night when I was asleep Satan tempted me with a
violence which I will remember as long as I am in this body. He fell on
me like a great rock and I could not stir a limb. How did it occur to
me in my ignorance to call on Elijah? Meanwhile I saw the sun rising
in the sky, and while I was shouting 'Elijah! Elijah!' at the top of my
voice the brilliance of that sun fell suddenly on me and lifted my
depression at once. I believe that I was sustained by Christ my Lord
and that his Spirit was even then calling out on my behalf. I hope this
is how it will be in my time of trouble, as he said in the Gospel. On
that day, the Lord declares, *it is not you who speak, but the Spirit of your
Father speaking through you.*

Final escape

[21] And so it was that, after many years, I was taken captive again. On
my first night among my captors I received a divine message which
said: 'You will be with them for two months.' That is just what
happened. On the sixtieth night the Lord rescued me from their
hands.

ut hodie cibum mittat uobis in uiam uestram usque dum satiamini, quia ubique abundabat illi'. Et adiuuante Deo ita factum est: ecce grex porcorum in uia ante oculos nostros apparuit, et multos ex illis interfecerunt et ibi duas noctes manserunt et bene refecti, et carne eorum repleti sunt, quia multi ex illis 'defecerunt' et secus uiam 'semiuiui relicti' sunt, et post hoc summas gratias egerunt Deo et ego honorificatus sum sub oculis eorum, et ex hac die cibum abundanter habuerunt; etiam 'mel siluestre' inuenerunt, et 'mihi partem obtulerunt' et unus ex illis dixit, 'Immolaticium est'. Deo gratias, exinde nihil gustaui.

20 Eadem uero nocte eram dormiens et fortiter temptauit me Satanas, quod memor ero 'quamdiu fuero in hoc corpore', et cecidit super me ueluti saxum ingens et nihil membrorum meorum praeualens. Sed unde me uenit ignaro in spiritu ut Heliam uocarem? Et inter haec uidi in caelum solem oriri et dum clamarem 'Helia, Helia' uiribus meis, ecce splendor solis illius decidit super me et statim discussit a me omnem grauitudinem, et credo quod a Xpisto Domino meo subuentus sum et Spiritus eius iam tunc clamabat pro me et spero quod sic erit 'in die pressurae' meae, sicut in euangelio inquit 'In illa die', Dominus testatur, 'non uos estis qui loquimini, sed Spiritus Patris uestri qui loquitur in uobis'.

21 Et iterum post annos multos adhuc capturam dedi. Ea nocte prima itaque mansi cum illis. 'Responsum' autem 'diuinum' audiui dicentem mihi 'Duobus mensibus eris cum illis'. Quod ita factum est: nocte illa sexagesima 'liberauit me Dominus de manibus eorum'.

go gcuirfidh sé bhur sáith bia chugaibh inniu mar tá go leor aige achan áit.' Agus le cuidiú Dé sin mar a tharla. I dtobainne tháinig tréad muc an bealach os ár gcomhair amach; mharaigh siad go leor acu agus d'fhanamar ansin ar feadh dhá oíche. Bhí siad beathaithe go maith agus d'ith siad a sáith muiceola nó bhí mórán acu traochta agus fágtha leath-mharbh ar an bhóthar. Ina dhiaidh sin thug siad buíochas mór do Dhia agus shíl siad a mhór domsa. Ón lá sin amach bhí go leor bia acu. Fiú amháin fuair siad mil fhiáin agus d'ofráil siad cuid domsa. Dúirt duine acu: 'Tá sí seo á hofráil duit mar íobairt.' Buíochas do Dhia níor bhlais mé a dhath di.

20 An oíche chéanna nuair a bhí mé i mo chodladh chuir Sátan cathú tíoránta orm a mbeidh cuimhne agam air a fhad agus a bheidh mé sa cholainn seo. Thit sé anuas orm mar a dhéanfadh carraig mhór agus ní thiocfadh liom ball de mo chorp a bhogadh. Agus caidé mar smaointigh mé air, aineolach agus mar bhí mé, glaoch ar Éilias. Idir an dá linn chonaic mé an ghrian ag éirí sa spéir agus nuair a bhí mé ag scairteadh 'Éilias, Éilias' in ard mo ghutha, thóg áilleacht na gréine mé gan mhoill as an ghruaim a bhí orm. Creidim gurbh é Críost mo Thiarna a chuidigh liom agus go raibh a spiorad ag glaoch amach ar mo shon. Tá súil agam gur sin mar a bheidh in uair na hanachaine mar a dúirt sé sa Soiscéal. Ar an lá sin, deir an Tiarna, *ní tusa a labhraíonn ach Spiorad an Athar a labhraíonn tríotsa.*

21 Mar sin, i ndiaidh mórán blianta, a gabhadh arís mé. An chéad oíche a bhí mé ina measc chuala mé teachtaireacht dhiaga á rá liom: 'Beidh tú leo go ceann dhá mhí.' Sin go díreach mar a tharla. Ar an seascú oíche d'fhuascail an Tiarna mé óna ngreim.

[22] As well as food for the journey he also gave us fire and dry weather every day until we met people ten days later. As I said above, we were in all twenty-eight days travelling through deserted country and the night we met people we had not a pick of food left.

Call of the Irish

On [23] another occasion, a few years later, I was in Britain with my relatives who welcomed me a son and earnestly begged me that I should never leave them, especially in view of all the hardships I had endured. It was there one night I saw the vision of a man called Victor, who appeared to have come from Ireland with an unlimited number of letters. He gave me one of them and I read the opening words which were: 'The voice of the Irish.' As I read the beginning of the letter I seemed at the same moment to hear the voice of those who were by the wood of Voclut which is near the Western Sea. They shouted with one voice: 'We ask you, holy boy, come and walk once more among us.' I was cut to the heart and could read no more, and so I learned by experience. Thank God, after very many years the Lord answered their cry.

Prayer of the Saviour

[24] Another night – whether in me or beside me I do not know, God knows – I was called in the most learned language which I heard but could not understand, except for the following statement at the end of the prayer: 'He who gave his life for you, he it is who is speaking in you.' At that I awoke full of joy.

[22] Etiam in itinere praeuidit nobis cibum et ignem et siccitatem cotidie donec decimo die peruenimus homines. Sicut superius insinuaui, uiginti et octo dies per desertum iter fecimus et ea nocte qua peruenimus homines de cibo uero nihil habuimus.

[23] Et iterum post paucos annos in Brittanniis eram cum parentibus meis, qui me ut filium susceperunt et ex fide rogauerunt me ut uel modo ego post tantas tribulationes quas ego pertuli nusquam ab illis discederem, et ibi scilicet 'uidi in uisu noctis' uirum uenientem quasi de Hiberione, cui nomen Uictoricius, cum epistolis innumerabilibus, et dedit mihi unam ex his et legi principium epistolae continentem 'Uox Hiberionacum', et cum recitabam principium epistolae putabam ipso momento audire uocem ipsorum qui erant iuxta siluam Uocluti quae est prope mare occidentale, et sic exclamauerunt 'quasi ex uno ore' 'Rogamus te, sancte puer, ut uenias et adhuc ambulas inter nos' et ualde 'compunctus sum corde' et amplius non potui legere et sic expertus sum. Deo gratias, quia post plurimos annos praestitit illis Dominus secundum clamorem illorum. [24] Et alia nocte, 'nescio, Deus scit', utrum in me an iuxta me, uerbis peritissimis, quos ego audiui et non potui intellegere, nisi ad postremum orationis sic effitiatus est '"Qui dedit animam suam pro te" ipse est qui loquitur in te' et sic expergefactus sum gaudibundus.

[22] Chomh maith le bia a thabhairt dúinn don turas thug sé aimsir mhaith agus ábhar tine dúinn achan lá go dtí gur bhuaileamar le daoine ar an deichiú lá. Mar a dúirt mé cheana, bhíomar ocht lá is fiche ag taisteal tríd an fhásach agus ní raibh greim bia fágtha againn an oíche ar casadh na daoine orainn.

[23] Uair eile, cúpla bliain ina dhiaidh sin, bhí mé sa Bhreatain le mo ghaolta. Chuir siad fáilte romham mar mhac agus d'impigh orm ó chroí gan iad a fhágáil choíche arís, go háirithe de bharr an cruatan ar fad a d'fhulaing mé. Ba ansin oíche amháin a chonaic mé i bhfís fear darbh ainm Victoricius, mar a bheadh sé ag teacht as Éirinn agus moll litreacha gan áireamh leis. Thug sé ceann acu dom agus léigh mé na chéad fhocail 'Glór na nGael'. Nuair a bhí mé ag léamh tús na litreach shíl mé ar an bhomaite sin gur chuala mé a nglór siúd a raibh cónaí orthu taobh le Coill Fhochlaid atá gar don Mhuir Thiar. Ghlaoigh siad orm in aon ghuth: 'Impímid ort, a ghasúir naofa, teacht agus siúl inár measc uair amháin eile.' Bhí mé croíbhriste agus ní raibh mé ábalta a thuilleadh a léamh. Agus ba chiall cheannaithe dom é. Buíochas do Dhia, i ndiaidh mórán blianta thug an Tiarna freagra ar a n-urnaí.

[24] Oíche eile, cé acu istigh ionam nó ag mo thaobh níl a fhios agam, ag Dia atá a fhios, cuireadh scairt orm i dteanga an-léannta a chuala mé ach a bhí dothuigthe agam seachas an ráiteas seo ag deireadh na hurnaí: 'An té a thug a anam ar do shon, eisean atá ag labhairt ionat.' Leis sin mhúscail mé agus mé lán áthais.

Prayer of the Spirit

[25] On yet another occasion I saw a person praying within me. I was as it seemed inside my body and I heard him over me, that is, over the inner man. There he was, praying with great emotion. All the time I was puzzled as I wondered greatly who could possibly be praying inside me. He spoke, however, at the end of the prayer, saying that he was the Spirit. In this way I learned by experience and I recalled the words of the apostle: *The Spirit helps the weaknesses of our prayer; for we do not know how to pray as we ought; but the Spirit himself pleads for us with sighs unutterable that cannot be put into words.* Again: *The Lord our Advocate pleads for us.*

The supreme test

[26] I was put on trial by a number of my seniors who came to cast up my sins as unfitting me for my laborious episcopate. On that day indeed the impulse was overpowering to fall away not only here and now but forever. But the Lord graciously spared his exile and wanderer for his own name's sake and helped me greatly when I was walked on in this way. As a result I did not come out of it badly, considering the disgrace and the blame I felt. I pray God that it may not be accounted to them as a sin.

[27] The charge against me which they discovered, after thirty years, was a confession which I had made before I became a deacon. In the anxiety of my troubled mind I confided to my dearest friend what I had done in my boyhood one day, in one hour indeed, because I had not yet overcome my sinful ways. God knows – I don't – whether I was yet fifteen. I did not believe in the living God, nor did I from childhood, but remained in death and unbelief until I was severely punished. I was well and truly humbled by hunger and nakedness and that every day.

[25] Et iterum uidi in me ipsum orantem et eram quasi intra corpus meum et audiui super me, hoc est super 'interiorem hominem', et ibi fortiter orabat gemitibus, et inter haec 'stupebam et admirabam et cogitabam' quis esset qui in me orabat, sed ad postremum orationis sic effitiatus est ut sit Spiritus, et sic expertus sum et recordatus sum apostolo dicente 'Spiritus adiuuat infirmitates orationis nostrae: nam quod oremus sicut oportet nescimus, sed ipse Spiritus postulat pro nobis gemitibus inenarrabilibus, quae uerbis exprimi non possunt'; et iterum 'Dominus aduocatus noster postulat pro nobis'.

[26] Et quando temptatus sum ab aliquantis senioribus meis, qui uenerunt et peccata mea contra laboriosum episcopatum meum obiecerunt, utique illo die fortiter 'impulsus sum ut caderem' hic et in aeternum; sed Dominus pepercit proselito et peregrino propter nomen suum benigne et ualde mihi subuenit in hac conculcatione. Quod in labe et in obprobrium non male deueni. Deum oro ut 'non illis in peccatum reputetur'.

[27] 'Occasionem' post annos triginta 'inuenerunt me aduersus' uerbum quod confessus fueram antequam essem diaconus. Propter anxietatem maesto animo insinuaui amicissimo meo quae in pueritia mea una die gesseram, immo in una hora, quia necdum praeualebam. 'Nescio Deus scit', si habebam tunc annos quindecim, et Deum uiuum non credebam neque ex infantia mea, sed in morte et in incredulitate mansi donec ualde castigatus sum 'et in ueritate humiliatus sum fame et nuditate' et cotidie.

✦

[25] Agus arís uair eile chonaic mé duine ag guí istigh ionam. Bhí mé mar a bheinn i mo chorp istigh agus chuala mé é os mo cheann, 'sé sin, os ceann an duine inmheánaigh. Bhí sé ansin ag urnaí agus tocht mór ina ghlór. An t-am ar fad bhí mearbhall agus iontas an domhain orm cé a d'fhéadfadh a bheith ag guí istigh ionam. Labhair sé, áfach, ag deireadh na hurnaí ag rá gurbh eisean an Spiorad. Ba mar sin a d'fhoghlaim mé agus chuimhnigh mé ar fhocail an Aspail: *Cuidíonn an Spiorad le laige ár n-urnaí; mar níl a fhios againn caidé mar is cóir dúinn urnaí. Ach bíonn an Spiorad ag idirghuí ar ár son le hosnaí doráite nach féidir a chur i bhfocail.* Arís: *Déanann an Tiarna, ár n-abhcóide, idirghuí ar ár son.*

[26] Chuir dream de mo sheanóirí faoi thriall mé nuair a tháinig siad ag casadh fúm faoi mo pheacaí, nach raibh siad ag cur le m'easpagacht shaothrach. Ar an lá sin leoga bhí mé chomh briste gur dhóbair dom titim, ní amháin ar an toirt ach go deo. Ach spáráil an Tiarna go geanúil a dheoraí agus a sheachránaí ar son a ainm agus chuidigh sé go mór liom nuair a bhí mé mo chur faoi chois ar an dóigh seo. Ní ródhona a bhí mé dá bharr, d'ainneoin mé a bheith faoi náire agus locht. Guím Dia nár agraí sé orthu é mar pheaca.

[27] Ba í an choir a fuair siad i m'aghaidh, i ndiaidh tríocha bliain, scéal a bhí admhaithe agam sula ndearnadh deagánach dom. De bharr imní agus buaireamh intinne d'inis mé don chara ab fhearr a bhí agam rud a rinne mé in aon lá amháin, ní hea ach in aon uair an chloig amháin, mar nach raibh neart ionam go fóill. Ag Dia atá a fhios, níl agamsa, an raibh mé cúig bliana déag d'aois. Níor chreid mé i nDia beo, nó níor chreid ó m'óige ach mé ag caitheamh mo shaoil sa bhás agus sa díchreideamh go dtí gur cuireadh pionós trom orm. Tugadh céim síos mhór dom le hocras agus le nochtacht agus sin achan lá.

[28] Contrary to the case against me I went to Ireland only with reluctance and not until I was almost exhausted. All this was really to my advantage, for as a result I was purified by the Lord. He prepared me in a way which has improved me so much from my former condition that I now care and work for the salvation of others whereas then I did not even consider my own.

Final approval

[29] The night following my rejection by those mentioned above, I had a vision of the night. I saw before my face a writing that dishonoured me, and simultaneously I heard God's voice saying to me: 'We have seen with disapproval the face of the chosen one deprived of his good name.' He did not say 'you have disapproved' but 'we have disapproved', as if to include himself. As he says: *He who touches you is as one who touches the apple of my eye.*

[30] Thanks be to God who supported me in everything, that he did not hinder the project I had undertaken nor the task which Christ the Lord had taught me. Rather did I feel from him no insignificant power and my good standing was approved in the presence of God and the people. [31] For these reasons I say boldly that my conscience does not reproach me here or for the future. God is my witness that I have told no lies in my account to you.

[32] My only sorrow that we should have deserved to hear such a report is for my dearest friend. To him I had confided my very soul. Before that interdiction I was told by some of the brothers that he would stand up for me in my absence. I was not there myself, nor was I even in Britain, nor did his intervention originate from me. He it was who had said to me in person; 'Look, you are going to be raised to the rank of bishop', although I was unworthy. How then did it occur to him afterwards to let me down publicly before all, good and bad, over something that he had previously granted me freely and gladly? And not he alone but the Lord also who is greater than all?

²⁸ Contra, Hiberione non sponte pergebam 'donec' prope 'deficiebam'; sed hoc potius bene mihi fuit, qui ex hoc emendatus sum a Domino et aptauit me ut hodie essem quod aliquando longe a me erat, ut ego curam haberem aut satagerem pro salute aliorum quando autem tunc etiam de me ipso non cogitabam.

²⁹ Igitur in illo die quo 'reprobatus sum' a memoratis supradictis ad noctem illam 'uidi in uisu noctis' quod scriptum erat contra faciem meam sine honore, et inter haec audiui 'responsum diuinum' dicentem mihi 'Male uidimus faciem designati nudato nomine', nec sic praedixit, 'male uidisti' sed 'male uidimus' quasi sibi me iunxisset sicut dixit 'Qui uos tangit quasi qui tangit pupillam oculi mei.'

³⁰ Idcirco 'gratias ago ei qui me' in omnibus 'confortauit,' ut non me impediret a profectione quam statueram et de mea quoque opera quod a Xpisto Domino meo didiceram, sed magis ex eo 'sensi in me uirtutem' non paruam et fides mea probata est coram Deo et hominibus. ³¹ Unde autem 'audenter dico' non me reprehendit conscientia mea hic et in futurum: 'teste Deo' habeo 'quia non sum mentitus' in sermonibus quos ego retuli uobis.

³² Sed magis doleo pro amicissimo meo cur hoc meruimus audire tale responsum. Cui ego credidi etiam animam. Et comperi ab aliquantis fratribus ante defensionem illam, quod ego non interfui nec in Brittanniis eram nec a me oriebatur, ut et ille in mea absentia pulsaret pro me; etiam mihi ipse ore suo dixerat 'Ecce dandus es tu ad gradum episcopatus', quod non eram dignus. Sed unde uenit illi postmodum ut coram cunctis, bonis et malis, et me publice dehonestaret quod ante sponte et laetus indulserat, et Dominus, qui 'maior omnibus est'?

²⁸ Murab ionann agus an cúiseamh seo, ní uaim féin a chuaigh mé go hÉirinn agus ní dhearna mé é sin go raibh mé chóir a bheith traochta. Ach bhí sé seo uilig chun mo leasa nó cheartaigh an Tiarna mé dá thairbhe. D'ullmhaigh sé mé ar dhóigh a chuir feabhas chomh mór sin orm ó mar bhí mé roimhe sin go bhfuil mé anois ag tabhairt cúraim agus ag obair do shlánú daoine eile, mise nár smaointigh orm féin uair amháin.

²⁹ An oíche i ndiaidh an mhuintir thuasluaite mé a dhiúltú, bhí fis agam san oíche. Chonaic mé os mo chomhair scríbhinn a chuir míchlú orm agus san am chéanna chuala mé glór Dé a rá liom: 'Chonaiceamar agus míshásamh orainn aghaidh an té a toghadh agus míchlú ar a ainm.' Níor dhúirt sé: 'bhí míshásamh ort' ach' bhí míshásamh orainn', mar a bheadh sé á chur féin san áireamh. Mar a deir sé: *An té a dhéanann teagmháil leat, tá sé mar an té a dhéanann teagmháil le mac imrisc mo shúile.*

³⁰ Buíochas do Dhia a chuidigh liom in achan rud agus nár chuir isteach orm leis an togra ar thug mé faoi nó an tasc a theagaisc Críost ár dTiarna dom. Ach a mhalairt nó mheas mé go raibh neart nach beag faighte agam uaidh agus dearbhaíodh do mo stádas i láthair Dé agus an phobail. ³¹ Dá bhrí sin deirim go dána nach ngoilleann mo chonsias orm anois agus nach ngoillfidh san am atá le teacht. Is é Dia an fhianaise nár inis mé bréaga ar bith ins an chuntas a thug mé daoibh.

³² Is mó mo bhrón faoin chara ab fhearr a bhí agam gur thuilleamar a leithéid de thuairisc a chluinstin. Dósan a d'inis mé rún mo chroí. Roimh an urghaire sin d'inis cuid de na bráithre dom go ndéanfadh sé mé a chosaint agus mé as láthair. Ní raibh mé ansin mé féin, nó ní raibh mé fiú sa Bhreatain, nó ní mise a spreag é i dtús ama. Ba é a dúirt sé liom lena bhéal féin: 'Amharc, ní mór tú a ardú go céim na heaspagachta' cé nach raibh sé tuillte agam. Ach caidé a tharla dó ina dhiaidh sin go ligfeadh sé síos go poiblí mé os comhair achan duine, maith is olc, de bharr oifig a bhí bronnta aige orm roimhe seo go fonnmhar agus dá dheoin féin. Agus ní amháin eisean ach an Tiarna atá níos mó ná aon duine?

³³ Enough said. But I cannot hide the gift of God which he gave me in the land of my captivity. I sought him vigorously then and there I found him. I am convinced that he kept me from all evil because of his Spirit who lives in me and has worked in me up to this day. I am speaking boldly again. But God knows if a mere man had said this to me it may be that I would have held my tongue out of Christian charity.

Prayer of thanksgiving

³⁴ I give thanks to my God tirelessly who kept me faithful in the day of trial, so that today I offer sacrifice to him confidently, the living sacrifice of my life to Christ, my Lord, who preserved me in all my troubles. I can say therefore: Who am I, Lord, and what is my calling that you should cooperate with me with such divine power? Today, among heathen peoples, I praise and proclaim your name in all places, not only when things go well but also in times of stress. Whether I receive good or ill, I return thanks equally to God, who taught me always to trust him unreservedly. His answer to my prayer inspired me in these latter days to undertake this holy and wonderful work in spite of my ignorance, and to imitate in some way those who, as the Lord foretold, would preach his Good News as a witness to all nations before the end of the world. We saw it that way and it happened that way. We are indeed witnesses that the Good News has been preached in distant parts, in places beyond which nobody lives.

Success due to God

Now ³⁵ it would take too long to relate all my labour, item by item or even in part. Let me tell you briefly how the most gracious God often freed me from slavery; how he rescued me twelve times when my life was in danger,

³³ Satis 'dico'. Sed tamen non debeo abscondere 'donum Dei' quod largitus est nobis 'in terra captiuitatis meae', quia tunc fortiter inquisiui eum et ibi inueni illum et seruauit me ab omnibus iniquitatibus, sic credo, 'propter inhabitantem Spiritum' eius, qui 'operatus est' usque in hanc diem in me. 'Audenter' rursus. Sed scit Deus si mihi homo hoc effatus fuisset, forsitan tacuissem propter 'caritatem Xpisti'.

³⁴ Unde ergo indefessam gratiam ago Deo meo qui me fidelem seruauit 'in die temptationis' meae, ita ut hodie confidenter offeram illi sacrificium ut 'hostiam uiuentem' animam meam Xpisto Domino meo, qui me 'seruauit ab omnibus angustiis meis' ut et dicam 'Quis ego sum, Domine', uel quae est uocatio mea, qui mihi tanta diuinitate comparuisti, ita ut hodie 'in gentibus' constanter 'exaltarem et magnificarem nomen tuum' ubicumque loco fuero, nec non in secundis sed etiam in pressuris, ut quicquid mihi euenerit siue bonum siue malum aequaliter debeo suscipere et Deo gratias semper agere, qui mihi ostendit ut indubitabilem eum sine fine crederem et qui me audierit ut ego inscius et 'in nouissimis diebus' hoc opus tam pium et tam mirificum auderem adgredere, ita ut imitarem quippiam illos quos ante Dominus iam olim praedixerat praenuntiaturos euangelium suum 'in testimonium omnibus gentibus' ante 'finem mundi', quod ita ergo uidimus itaque suppletum est. Ecce testes sumus quia euangelium praedicatum est usque ubi nemo ultra est.

³⁵ Longum est autem totum per singula enarrare laborem meum uel per partes. Breuiter dicam qualiter piissimus Deus de seruitute saepe liberauit et de periculis duodecim qua periclitata est anima mea

³³ Tá go leor ráite. Ach ní féidir liom an tíolacadh a bhronn Dia orm i dtír mo dhaoirse a cheilt. Chuaigh mé á lorg le dúthracht agus ba ansin a fuair mé é. Tá mé den bharúil gur choinnigh sé ó achan olc mé de bharr a spiorad atá lonnaithe ionam agus atá ag obair ionam go dtí an lá inniu féin. Tá mé ag labhairt go dána arís. Ach ag Dia atá a fhios dá mba duine a déarfadh é seo liom, b'fhéidir go bhfanfainn i mo thost as ucht grá Chríost. ³⁴ Bheirim buíochas de shíor do mo Dhia a choinnigh dílis mé lá mo chathaithe sa dóigh go dtig liom íobairt a ofráil go muiníneach inniu dó, beo-íobairt mo shaoil do Chríost mo Thiarna a chaomhnaigh mé ó mo thrioblóidí go léir. Thig liom a rá mar sin: Cé mé féin, a Thiarna, agus cén glaoch atá agam gur chóir do do neart diaga a bheith ag comhoibriú liom? Inniu, i measc mórán págánach, molaim agus fógraím d'ainm achan áit, ní amháin nuair atá rudaí ag dul go maith ach fosta in am na teannais. Cé acu a éiríonn go maith nó go holc liom, bheirim mór-bhuíochas do Dhia a mhúin i gcónaí dom muinín a bheith amach is amach agam ann. Spreag a fhreagra ar mo phaidir mé ins na laethanta deiridh sin tabhairt faoin obair iontach, bheannaithe sin d'ainneoin m'aineolais, agus aithris a dhéanamh ar dhóigh éigin orthu seo, mar a chuir an Tiarna in iúl roimh ré, a chraobhscaoilfeadh an Soiscéal mar fhianaise do na náisiúin uilig go dtí críocha an domhain. Chonaiceamar mar sin é agus sin mar a tharla sé. Táimidne, leoga, mar fhianaise go bhfuil an Soiscéal á chraobhscaoileadh in áiteanna scoite ó chónaí ar bith daoine. ³⁵ Anois ghlacfadh sé rófhada cur síos ar mo shaothar uilig, eachtra i ndiaidh eachtra nó ina chodanna. Inseoidh mé i mbeagán focal caidé mar a shaor Dia na mór-thrócaire mé ón daoirse; caidé mar a thug sé tarrtháil orm dhá uair déag nuair a bhí mo shaol i mbaol,

as well as from numerous conspiracies and things which I cannot put into words. I do not wish to bore my readers; but God, who knows all things in advance, is my witness that he used to forewarn me often by a divine message, poor orphan and ignorant as I was.

[36] How did I come by this wisdom which was not my own, I who neither knew what was in store for me, nor what it was to relish God? What was the source of the gift I got later, the great and beneficial gift of knowing and loving God, even if it meant leaving my homeland and my relatives?

[37] Many gifts were offered to me in sorrow and tears. I offended the donors and also some of my seniors against my wishes. Under the guidance of God in no way did I agree or give in to them. It was not I but the grace of God who overcame in me and resisted all those things. I came to the Irish heathens to preach the Good News and to put up with insults from unbelievers. I heard my travelling mission put down, I endured many persecutions even to the extent of chains, I gave up my free-born status for the good of others. Should I be worthy I am ready to give even my life, promptly and gladly, for his name's sake; and it is there that I wish to spend it until I die, if the Lord should grant it to me.

[38] I am very much in debt to God, who gave me so much grace that through me many people should be born again in God and afterwards confirmed, and that clergy should be ordained for them everywhere. All this was for a people newly come to belief whom the Lord took from the very ends of the earth as he promised long ago, through his prophets: *To you the nations will come from the uttermost parts of the earth and say: 'Our fathers got for themselves worthless idols, and there is no profit in them'*. And again: *I have set you to be a light for the Gentiles, that you may bring salvation to the uttermost parts of the earth.*

praeter insidias multas et 'quae uerbis exprimere non ualeo'. Nec iniuriam legentibus faciam, sed Deum auctorem habeo, qui nouit omnia etiam antequam fiant. ut me pauperculum pupillum idiotam 'responsum diuinum' crebre admonere.
[36] 'Unde mihi haec sapientia', quae in me non erat, qui nec 'numerum dierum noueram' neque Deum sapiebam? Unde mihi postmodum donum tam magnum tam salubre Deum agnoscere uel diligere, sed ut patriam et parentes amitterem?
[37] Et munera multa mihi offerebantur cum fletu et lacrimis et offendi illos, nec non contra uotum aliquantos de senioribus meis, sed gubernante Deo nullo modo consensi neque adquieui illis, non mea gratia, sed Deus qui uincit in me et resistit illis omnibus, ut ego ueneram ad Hibernas gentes euangelium praedicare et ab incredulis contumelias perferre, ut 'audirem obprobrium peregrinationis meae', et persecutiones multas 'usque ad uincula' et ut darem ingenuitatem meam pro utilitate aliorum et, si dignus fuero, 'promptus' sum ut etiam 'animam meam' incunctanter et 'libentissime' pro nomine eius. Et ibi opto 'impendere' eam 'usque ad mortem' si Dominus mihi indulgeret, [38] quia ualde 'debitor sum' Deo, qui mihi tantam gratiam donauit ut populi multi per me in Deum renascerentur et postmodum consummarentur et ut clerici ubique illis ordinarentur ad plebem nuper uenientem ad credulitatem, quam sumpsit Dominus 'ab extremis terrae', sicut olim promiserat per prophetas suos: 'Ad te gentes uenient ab extremis terrae et dicent, "Sicut falsa comparauerunt patres nostri idola et non est in eis utilitas"' et iterum 'Posui te lumen in gentibus ut sis in salutem usque ad extremum terrae'.

chomh maith le go leor comhchealg agus rudaí do-inste. Ní mian liom mo chuid léitheoirí a chrá, ach is é Dia, a bhfuil a fhios aige gach rud fiú sula dtarlaíonn sé, m'fhianaise gur ghnách leis roimh ré trí theachtaireacht dhiaga comhairle a chur ormsa, an dílleachta bocht aineolach.
[36] Caidé mar a fuair mise an eagna seo nach raibh ionam féin, mise narbh eol dom uimhir mo laethanta agus nach bhfuair blas ar Dhia? Caidé an fhoinse as ar tháinig an tíolacadh a fuair mé níos moille, an tíolacadh mór tairbheach aithne a chur ar Dhia agus grá a thabhairt dó, fiú dá gcaillfinn mo thír dhúchais agus mo ghaolta dá bharr?
[37] hOfráladh mórán bronntanas dom faoi bhrón agus na deora leo. Mhaslaigh mé iad agus cuid de mo sheanóirí i gcoinne mo thola. Faoi threoir Dé níor aontaigh mé leo nó níor ghéill mé dóibh ar dhóigh ar bith. Níorbh é mo ghrásta ach Dia a fuair an bua ionam agus a sheas an fód ina n-aghaidh. Tháinig mé go dtí na págánaigh in Éirinn leis an Soiscéal a chraobhscaoileadh agus cur suas le maslaí ón dream sin nár chreid. Chuala mé mo mhisean a cháineadh agus d'fhulaing mé mórán géarleanúna go fiú a bheith i gcuibhreacha agus thug mé suas mo stádas saorchlannda ar mhaithe le daoine eile. Agus más fiú mé tá mé réidh m'anam a thabhairt láithreach le fonn agus le háthas ar son a ainm. Agus is ansin is mian liom mo shaol a chaitheamh go bás má cheadaíonn an Tiarna dom é. [38] Tá mé go mór faoi chomaoin ag Dia a thug an méid sin grásta dom gur athghineadh i nDia tríom na sluaite daoine ar cóineartaíodh iad ina dhiaidh sin agus gur oirníodh sagairt dóibh achan áit. Bhí sé seo fá choinne pobail nár tháinig chun an chreidimh ach le goirid, pobal a thug an Tiarna ó chríocha na cruinne mar a gheall sé fadó trína fháithe: *Tiocfaidh na náisiúin chugat ó cheithre airde na cruinne agus déarfaidh siad: Fuair ár n-aithreacha dóibh féin déithe bréige nach raibh aon tairbhe iontu.* Agus arís: *Tá tú ceaptha agam le bheith i do sholas do na náisiúin, ionas go mbeidh tú i d'údar slánaithe go críocha an domhain.*

Duty to preach the Gospel

[39] I wish to wait there for the promise of one who never breaks his word, as he promises in the Gospel: *They will come from east and the west and sit at table with Abraham and Isaac and Jacob,* just as we believe the faithful will come from every part of the world. [40] For that reason we ought to fish well and diligently in accordance with the advice and teaching of the Lord, who says: *Follow me, and I will make you fishers of men.* There are also the words of the prophets: *Behold, I am sending fishers and many hunters, says God;* and so on.

It was then most necessary to spread out our nets so that a very great multitude might be caught for God and that there might be clergy everywhere to baptise and preach to a people in need and want. As the Lord says in the Gospel by way of exhorting and teaching: *Go therefore now, make disciples of all nations, baptising them in the name of the Father and of the Son and of the Holy Spirit, teaching them to observe all that I have commanded you; and lo, I am with you always, to the close of the age.* Again he says: *Go therefore into all the world and preach the Gospel to the whole creation. He who believes and is baptised will be saved; but he who does not believe will be condemned.* And again: *This Gospel of the kingdom will be preached throughout the whole world, as a testimony to all nations; and then the end will come.*

In the same way the Lord announces beforehand through the prophet: *And in the last days it shall be, God declares, that I will pour out my Spirit upon all flesh, and your sons and your daughters shall prophesy, your young men shall see visions, and your old men shall dream dreams; yea, and on my menservants and my maidservants in those days I will pour out my Spirit; and they shall prophesy.* In Hosea he says: *Those who are not my people I will call 'my people' and her who had not received mercy I will call 'her who has received mercy'. And in the very place where it was said, 'You are not my people', they will be called 'sons of the living God'.*

³⁹ Et ibi uolo 'expectare promissum' ipsius, qui utique numquam fallit, sicut in euangelio pollicetur: 'Uenient ab oriente et occidente et recumbent cum Abraham et Isaac et Iacob,' sicut credimus ab omni mundo uenturi sunt credentes. ⁴⁰ Idcirco itaque oportet quidem bene et diligenter piscare, sicut Dominus praemonet et docet dicens: 'Uenite post me et faciam uos fieri piscatores hominum' et iterum dicit per prophetas: 'Ecce mitto piscatores et uenatores multos, dicit Deus' et cetera. Unde autem ualde oportebat retia nostra tendere, ita ut 'multitudo copiosa et turba' Deo caperetur et ubique essent clerici qui baptizarent et exhortarent populum indigentem et desiderantem, sicut Dominus inquit in euangelio, admonet et docet dicens: 'Euntes ergo nunc docete omnes gentes baptizantes eas in nomine Patris et Filii et Spiritus Sancti docentes eos obseruare omnia quaecumque mandaui uobis: et ecce ego uobiscum sum omnibus diebus usque ad consummationem saeculi', et iterum dicit 'Euntes ergo in mundum uniuersum praedicate euangelium omni creaturae; qui crediderit et baptizatus fuerit saluus erit; qui uero non crediderit condempnabitur' et iterum 'Praedicabitur hoc euangelium regni in uniuerso mundo in testimonium omnibus gentibus et tunc ueniet finis' et item Dominus per prophetam praenuntiat, inquit 'Et erit in nouissimis diebus, dicit Dominus, effundam de Spiritu meo super omnem carnem et prophetabunt filii uestri et filiae uestrae et iuuenes uestri uisiones uidebunt et seniores uestri somnia somniabunt et quidem super seruos meos et super ancillas meas in diebus illis effundam de Spiritu meo et prophetabunt', et 'in Osee dicit, Uocabo non plebem meam plebem meam et non misericordiam consecutam misericordiam consecutam et erit in loco ubi dictum est, Non plebs mea uos, ibi uocabuntur filii Dei uiui.'

³⁹ Agus is ansin is mian liom fanacht le gealltanas ón té nach mbriseann a fhocal in am ar bith mar a gheallann sé sa Soiscéal: *Tiocfaidh siad anoir agus aniar agus suífidh siad ag an tábla le hAbrahám agus le hÍosác agus le Iacób*, de réir mar a chreidimid go bhfuil na fíréin ag teacht ó achan chearn den domhan. ⁴⁰ Dá bhrí sin is cóir dúinn iascaireacht mhaith dhícheallach a dhéanamh mar a chomhairlíonn agus a mhúineann an Tiarna a deir: *Leanaigí mé agus déanfaidh mé iascairí ar dhaoine daoibh.* Agus deir sé arís trí na fáithe: *Féach, tá mé ag cur iascairí agus mórán sealgairí, a deir Dia,* agus araile. Dá bhrí sin bhí sé an-riachtanach ár gcuid eangacha a spré amach sa dóigh go ngabhfaí slua mór daoine do Dhia agus go mbeadh cléir achan áit leis na daoine a bhí in easpa agus ag tnúth leis an bhaisteadh agus seanmóireacht a dhéanamh dóibh. Mar a deir an Tiarna sa Soiscéal, ag tabhairt comhairle agus ag teagasc: *Imigí libh anois; déanaigí deisceabail de na náisiúin uilig, á mbaisteadh in ainm an Athar agus an Mhic agus an Spioraid Naoimh, ag múineadh dóibh achan rud a d'ordaigh mé daoibh a chomhlíonadh. Agus féach, tá mé libh i gcónaí go deireadh an tsaoil.* Arís deir sé: *Gabhaigí amach mar sin ar fud an domhain, fógraigí an Soiscéal ar fud na cruinne. An té a chreidfidh agus a bhaistfear, slánófar é agus an té nach gcreidfidh daorfar é.* Agus arís: *Fógrófar Soiscéal seo na ríochta ar fud an domhain mhóir mar fhianaise do na náisiúin uilig, agus ansin tiocfaidh an deireadh.* Ar an dóigh céanna d'fhógair an Tiarna roimh ré tríd an bhfáidh: *Ins na laethanta deireanacha, fógraíonn an Tiarna, doirtfidh mé amach mo Spiorad ar an uile dhuine, agus déanfaidh bhur gclannmhac agus bhur n-iníonacha tairngreacht. Tchífidh na fir óga aislingí agus beidh na fir aosta ag brionglóidigh. Doirtfidh mé amach mo Spiorad ins na laethanta seo ar mo shearbhóntaí fear agus ban, agus déanfaidh siad tairngreacht.* Agus in Óseá deir sé: *glaofaidh mé 'mo phobal' ar an phobal nach liom, agus 'ise a fuair trócaire' ar an té nach bhfuair trócaire. Agus ins an áit ar dúradh: 'ní muintir liom sibhse' glaofar orthu siúd 'clann Dé bhí'.*

Fervour of Irish converts

[41] How, then, does it happen in Ireland that a people who in their ignorance of God always worshipped only idols and unclean things up to now, have lately become a people of the Lord and are called children of God? How is it that the sons and daughters of Scoto-Irish chieftains are seen to be monks and virgins dedicated to Christ?

[42] There was, in particular, a virtuous Scoto-Irish woman of noble birth and great beauty, already grown to womanhood. I had baptised her myself. A few days later she came to us with a purpose, to tell us that she had been advised, in a divine message, to become a virgin of Christ and to draw close to God. Thanks be to God, six days later she carried this out in the most excellent and enthusiastic way. So too, all the virgins. Their fathers disapprove of them, so they often suffer persecution and unfair abuse from their families; yet their number goes on increasing. Indeed, the number of virgins from our own race who were born there is beyond counting, and to these must be added the widows and those who forego their marriage rights. Of them all the women who live in slavery suffer the most. They have to endure terror and threats all the time. But the Lord has given grace to many of his handmaids and, although they are forbidden, they follow him steadfastly.

Human problems

[43] What if I should consider leaving them and going to Britain? How dearly would I love to go, like a man going to his homeland and relatives, and not only there but also to Gaul in order to visit the brothers and to see the face of the saintly ones of my Lord! God knows how much I yearned for it, but I am tied by the Spirit. He makes it clear to me that if I do this he will hold me responsible for the future and I am afraid of undoing the work which I have begun. It was not really I but Christ the Lord who commanded me to come here and to stay with them for the rest of my life. The Lord willing, he will protect me from everything that is evil so that I may commit no sin against him.

41 Unde autem Hiberione qui numquam notitiam Dei habuerunt nisi idola et inmunda usque nunc semper coluerunt quomodo 'nuper facta est plebs Domini' et filii Dei nuncupantur, filii Scottorum et filiae regulorum monachi et uirgines Xpisti esse uidentur? 42 Et etiam una benedicta Scotta genetiua nobilis pulcherrima adulta erat, quam ego baptizaui, et post paucos dies una causa uenit ad nos, insinuauit nobis responsum accepisse a nuntio Dei et monuit eam ut esset uirgo Xpisti et ipsa Deo proximaret: Deo gratias, sexta ab hac die optime et auidissime arripuit illud quod etiam omnes uirgines Dei ita hoc faciunt, non sponte patrum earum, sed et persecutiones patiuntur et improperia falsa a parentibus suis et nihilominus plus augetur numerus, et de genere nostro qui ibi nati sunt, nescimus numerum eorum, praeter uiduas et continentes. Sed et illae maxime laborant quae seruitio detinentur, usque ad terrores et minas assidue perferunt; sed Dominus gratiam dedit multis ex ancillis suis, nam etsi uetantur tamen fortiter imitantur.

43 Unde autem etsi uoluero amittere illas et ut pergens in Brittanniis, et libentissime 'paratus eram' quasi ad patriam et parentes; non id solum sed etiam usque ad Gallias uisitare fratres et ut uiderem faciem sanctorum Domini mei; scit Deus quod ego ualde optabam, sed 'alligatus Spiritu', qui mihi 'protestatur' si hoc fecero, ut futurum reum me esse designat et timeo perdere laborem quem inchoaui, et non ego sed Xpistus Dominus, qui me imperauit ut uenirem esse cum illis residuum aetatis meae, 'si Dominus uoluerit' et custodierit me ab omni via mala, ut non 'peccem coram illo'.

⊕

41 Caidé mar a tharla sé in Éirinn daoine a bhí ariamh gan eolas ar Dhia ach iad i gcónaí go dtí seo ag adhradh íol agus nithe míghlana, caidé mar a tharla sé go ndearnadh pobal an Tiarna díobh ar na mallaibh agus go dtugtar clann De orthu anois? Caidé mar a tharla sé go bhfuil clannmhac na Scotach agus iníonacha na ríthe le feiceáil ina manaigh agus ina maighdeana ag Críost?

42 Bhí go áirithe cailín suáilceach Scotach amháin ann, de shíol uasal agus í fíor-álainn agus in aois mná, cailín a bhaist mé féin. Cúpla lá ina dhiaidh sin tháinig sí chugainn le haon aidhm amháin, lena insint dúinn go bhfuair sí comhairle ó theachtaire Dé a bheith ina maighdean ag Críost agus a theacht gar do Dhia. Buíochas do Dhia, sé lá ina dhiaidh sin, rinne sí sin faoi chroí mhór mhaith. Mar an gcéanna na maighdeana uilig. Ní aontaíonn a n-aithreacha leo agus is minic a bhíonn siad faoi ghéarleanúint agus faoi mhasla gan chúis óna dteaghlaigh. Ach d'ainneoin sin tá a líon ag méadú. Níl a fhios againn cá mhéad maighdeana dár gcine féin a rugadh ansin chomh maith le baintreacha agus lánúna a staonann óna gcearta pósta. Díobh seo is iad na bansclábhaithe is mó atá ag fulaingt. Bíonn siad faoi uamhan agus faoi bhagairt an t-am ar fad. Ach thug an Tiarna a ghrásta do mhórán dá bhanseirbhísigh; cé go gcrostar orthu, leanann siad a lorg go dílis.

43 Cad a tharlódh dá mba mhian liom iad a fhágáil agus dul chun na Breataine? Nach orm a bheadh an fonn imeachta, mar dhuine ag dul ar ais go dtí a bhaile dúchais agus a ghaolta, agus ní amháin ansin ach go dtí an Ghaill le cuairt a thabhairt ar na bráithre agus aghaidh na naomh Críostaí a fheiceáil. Ag Dia atá a fhios caidé chomh mór agus a bhí mé ag tnúth leis sin, ach tá ceangal ag an Spiorad orm. Cuireann sé in iúl dom dá ndéanfainn amhlaidh go gcuirfeadh sé an fhreagracht orm san am atá le teacht agus tá eagla orm an obair a thosaigh mé a chur ar ceal. Ní mise go díreach ach Críost a d'ordaigh dom a theacht anseo agus fanacht leo an chuid eile de mo shaol. Más é toil an Tiarna é, cosnóidh sé mé ó achan olc ionas nach ndéanfaidh mé peaca ina láthair.

[44] This, I hope, is my duty, but I do not trust myself as long as I am in this mortal body. Strong is the enemy who tries every day to turn me away from the faith and purity of that true religion to which I have devoted myself to the end of my life for Christ my Lord. My uncooperative body is forever dragging me towards death, that is, towards the satisfaction of unlawful desires, and I realise this partly because I have not altogether led a life as perfect as other believers. But I confess it to my Lord and I do not blush in his sight because I am not telling lies. From the time in my early manhood when I came to know him, the love of God and reverence for him have grown in me, and up to now, by the favour of God, I have kept the faith.

[45] Let him who wishes laugh and scoff. I do not intend to be silent, nor to conceal the signs and wonders that the Lord showed me many years before they happened, as befits him who knows everything, even before the beginning of time. [46] I must return unending thanks to God who often pardoned my folly and my carelessness, and on more than one occasion spared me his great wrath. Although he chose me to be his helper I was slow to accept the prompting of the Spirit. The Lord showed kindness to me a million times because he saw that I was ready, even if I did not know what to do about my position because of the number of people who were hindering my mission. They used to discuss me among themselves behind my back: 'Why does this fellow throw himself into danger among enemies who have no knowledge of God?' There was no malice on their part; they simply did not appreciate how my mission should be regarded on account of my lack of education, and I freely admit this myself. I failed myself to realise in good time the grace that was then in me. It is obvious to me now what I should have understood earlier.

⁴⁴ Spero autem hoc debueram, sed memet ipsum non credo 'quamdiu fuero in hoc corpore mortis', quia fortis est qui cotidie nititur subuertere me a fide et praeposita castitate religionis non fictae usque in finem uitae meae Xpisto Domino meo. sed 'caro inimica' semper trahit ad mortem. id est ad inlecebras inlicitate perficiendas; et 'scio ex parte' quare uitam perfectam ego non egi 'sicut' et 'ceteri' credentes, sed confiteor Domino meo. et non erubesco in conspectu ipsius 'quia non mentior' ex quo cognoui eum 'a iuuentute mea' creuit in me amor Dei et timor ipsius 'et usque nunc' fauente Domino 'fidem seruaui'.

⁴⁵ Rideat autem et insultet qui uoluerit, ego non silebo neque abscondo signa et mirabilia quae mihi a Domino monstrata sunt ante multos annos quam fierent, quasi qui nouit omnia etiam 'ante tempora saecularia'. ⁴⁶ Unde autem debueram sine cessatione Deo gratias agere, qui saepe indulsit insipientiae meae neglegentiae meae et de loco non in uno quoque ut non mihi uehementer irasceretur, qui adiutor datus sum et non cito adquieui secundum quod mihi ostensum fuerat et sicut 'Spiritus suggerebat' et 'misertus est' mihi Dominus 'in milia milium', quia uidit in me quod 'paratus eram', sed quod mihi pro his nesciebam de statu meo quid facerem, quia multi hanc legationem prohibebant, etiam inter se ipsos post tergum meum narrabant et dicebant 'Iste quare se mittit in periculo inter hostes qui Deum non nouerunt?' non ut causa malitiae, sed non sapiebat illis, sicut et ego ipse testor, intellige propter rusticitatem meam, et non cito agnoui gratiam quae tunc erat in me; nunc mihi sapit quod ante debueram.

⁴⁴ Tá súil agam gurb é seo mo dhualgas, ach níl muinín agam asam féin a fhad is atá mé sa chorp básmhar seo. Is láidir é an té atá ag iarraidh achan lá mé a mhealladh ón dílseacht agus ó gheanmnaíocht an fhíor-chreidimh a bhfuil mé doirte dó go deireadh mo shaoil ar son Chríost mo Thiarna. Tá an choileann naimhdeach seo de shíor ag mo tharraingt chun báis, 'sé sin, chun ainmhianta mídhleathacha a shásamh. Tuigim é seo sa mhéid nach raibh mo shaol gan locht nó chomh maith le daoine eile a chreid i nDia. Ach admhaím do Dhia agus ní bhíonn náire orm os a chomhair mar níl mé ag inse bréag. Ón am i dtús m'óige nuair a fuair mé eolas air, d'fhás grá Dé agus a umhlaíocht ionam, agus suas go dtí anois, le grásta Dé, choinnigh mé an creideamh.

⁴⁵ Is féidir leis an té ar mian leis a bheith ag gáire agus ag magadh. Ní mian liom a bheith i mo thost nó na comharthaí nó na hiontais a thaispeáin an Tiarna dom mórán blianta sular tharla siad, a cheilt, mar a oireann don té a bhfuil a fhios aige achan rud fiú ó thús ama. ⁴⁶ Caithfidh mé buíochas gan staonadh a thabhairt do Dhia a thug pardún dom go minic as mo chuid amaidí agus neamairt agus nár ghabh fearg mhór é liom níos mó ná uair amháin. Agus cé gur thogh sé mé le cuidiú leis, bhí mé mall ag glacadh le gríosadh an Spioraid. Agus léirigh an Tiarna a chineáltas dom na mílte mílte uair, mar chonaic sé go raibh mé réidh, fiú muna raibh a fhios agam caidé ba chóir a dhéanamh faoi mo chás as siocair an méid daoine a bhí ag cur isteach ar mo shaothar. Ba ghnách leo bheith ag cúlchaint fúm eatarthu féin: 'Cén fáth a gcuireann an boc seo é féin i gcontúirt i measc naimhde nach bhfuil eolas acu ar Dhia? Ní go mailíseach a bhí siad á rá seo; níor thuig siad caidé mar a dhéanfainn mo chuid oibre as siocair m'easpa oideachais, rud a thuigim féin. Níor thug mé féin faoi deara go luath an grásta a bhí ionam ag an am. An rud atá soiléir dom anois ba cheart dom é a aithint níos luaithe.

[47] Now I have given here a simple account of my brothers and fellow-servants. They believed me because of what I foretold and still foretell in order to strengthen and consolidate your faith. Would that you, too, would reach out to greater things and do better! This will be my happiness, because a *wise son is the glory of his father.*

Money matters

[48] You know, as does God, how I have behaved among you from my early manhood, with genuine faith and a sincere heart. I have equally kept faith with the heathens among whom I live and I will continue to keep it. God knows I have cheated none of them for the sake of God and his Church; nor would the thought occur to me, lest I should provoke persecution against them and against us all, or that through me the name of the Lord would be blasphemed. It is written: *Woe to the man through whom the name of the Lord is blasphemed.*

[49] Although I am unskilled in every way I have tried somehow to keep my reserve even from the Christian brethren and the virgins of Christ and the religious women who used to offer me little presents unasked. They would even leave some of their jewellery on the altar and when I insisted on giving them back they were offended. But mine was the long-term view and for that reason I used take every precaution so that the heathens might not catch me out on any grounds of infidelity concerning myself or the work of my ministry. I was unwilling to give unbelievers even the slightest opportunity for slander or disparagement. [50] When I baptised so many thousands, would I have expected even a penny from any of them? Tell me and I will give it back. Or when the Lord ordained through my insignificant person so many clergy and distributed the ministry to them free, did I ever ask of any of them even the price of a shoe? Speak up and I will return it.

⁴⁷ Nunc ergo simpliciter insinuaui fratribus et conseruis meis qui mihi crediderunt propter quod 'praedixi et praedico' ad roborandum et confirmandam fidem uestram. Utinam ut et uos imitemini maiora et potiora faciatis. Hoc erit gloria mea, quia 'filius sapiens gloria patris est'.
⁴⁸ Uos scitis et Deus, qualiter inter uos conversatus sum 'a iuuentute mea' in fide ueritatis 'et in sinceritate cordis'. Etiam ad gentes illas inter quas habito, ego fidem illis praestaui et praestabo. Deus scit 'neminem' illorum 'circumueni', nec cogito, propter Deum et ecclesiam ipsius, ne 'excitem' illis et nobis omnibus 'persecutionem' et ne per me blasphemaretur nomen Domini, quia scriptum est 'Uae homini per quem nomen Domini blasphematur'.
⁴⁹ Nam 'etsi imperitus sum in omnibus' tamen conatus sum quippiam seruare me etiam et fratribus Xpistianis et uirginibus Xpisti et mulieribus religiosis, quae mihi ultronea munuscula donabant et super altare iactabant ex ornamentis suis et iterum reddebam illis et aduersus me scandalizabantur cur hoc faciebam. Sed ego propter spem perennitatis, ut me in omnibus caute propterea conseruarem, ita ut non me in aliquo titulo infideli caperent uel ministerium seruitutis meae nec etiam in minimo incredulis locum darem infamare siue detractare. ⁵⁰ Forte autem quando baptizaui tot milia hominum sperauerim ab aliquo illorum uel dimidio scriptulae? 'Dicite mihi et reddam uobis.' Aut quando ordinauit ubique Dominus clericos per modicitatem meam et ministerium gratis distribui illis si poposci ab aliquo illorum uel pretium uel 'calciamenti' mei, 'dicite aduersus me et reddam uobis' magis.

⁴⁷ Anois tá cuntas ionraic tugtha agam do mo bhráithre agus mo chomhsheirbhísigh. Chreid siad mé de bharr an méid a thuar mé dóibh agus atá mé a thuar go fóill leis an chreideamh a neartú agus a dhaingniú. Nár dheas sibhse fosta a bheith ar thóir spriocanna níos airde agus nithe níos fearr. Seo í an ghlóir a bheidh agamsa, mar is *glóir athar é an mac eagnaí.*
⁴⁸ Tá a fhios agaibh mar atá a fhios ag Dia caidé mar a d'iompair mé mé féin in bhur measc le firinne chreidimh agus dúthracht chroí ó tháinig ann dom. Mar an gcéanna leis na págánaigh ar mhair mé ina measc, chuir mé le m'fhocal dóibh agus sin mar a bheas i gcónaí. Ag Dia atá a fhios nár fheall mé ar aon duine acu ar son Dé agus a eaglaise; ná ní chuimhneoinn air ar eagla go spreagfainn géarleanúint ina measc siúd agus inar measc uilig nó go dtabharfaí masla d'ainm an Tiarna tríomsa. Tá sé scríofa: *Is mairg don té gur tríd a dhéantar ainm an Tiarna a mhaslú.*
⁴⁹ Cé go bhfuil mé neamhoilte ar achan dóigh thug mé iarraidh mé féin a chosaint fiú ar na bráithre Críostaí, ar mhaighdeana Chríost agus ar na mná cráifeacha a d'ofráileadh dom bronntanais bheaga nár iarr mé orthu. D'fhágaidís cuid dá seoda ar an altóir agus nuair a thugainn ar ais dóibh iad, bhídís míshásta liom. Ach ba dhearcadh fadradharcach a bhí agam agus ar an ábhar sin ba ghnách liom a bheith an-chúramach nach mbeadh na págánaigh ábalta a chur i mo leith go raibh mídhílseacht ar bith ag baint liom féin nó leis an mhinistreacht. Ní raibh mé sásta an deis is lú a thabhairt d'ainchreidmhigh cúlchaint nó cáineadh a dhéanamh. ⁵⁰ Nuair a bhaist mé mórán mílte acu, an mbeinn ag súil le pingin amháin uathu? Inis dom agus bhéarfaidh mé ar ais é. Nó nuair a d'oirnigh an Tiarna cléirigh i ngach áit tríd an duine suarach seo agus gur bhronn mé an mhinistreacht orthu in aisce, má d'iarr mé luach mo bhróige riamh, labhraigí amach agus bhéarfaidh mé ar ais é.

51 On the contrary, I spent money in your interest that I might be accepted; I travelled among you and on your account exposed myself to many dangers everywhere, even in the most remote districts beyond which nobody lives and where nobody had ever come to baptise, to ordain clergy or to confirm the people. It was the Lord's gift to me that I undertook everything with concern and eagerness for your salvation. 52 All the while I used to give presents to the kings over and above the expenses I paid their sons who travel with me. Even so, on one occasion they abducted my companions and me, and were fanatically bent on killing me that day; but my time had not yet come. They made off with everything they got their hands on and put me in chains. Fourteen days later the Lord rescued me from their power and our belongings were returned through the offices of God and the good friends we had made previously. 53 You have had experience also of how much I paid the brehons in all the districts which I used to visit very often. I must have distributed not less than the honour-price of fifteen men among them in order that you might have the pleasure of my company and that I might always have the pleasure of yours until we meet God. I do not regret this; I do not consider it enough. I am still spending and will go on spending more. The Lord has power to allow me ultimately to spend myself in the interest of your souls.

Purity of motive

54 Look, I called upon God to witness by my life that I am not telling lies; that neither am I writing to you out of flattery or greed for money, nor because I look for esteem from any of you. Sufficient is the esteem that is not yet seen but that is felt in the heart. Faithful is he who made the promise; he never tells a lie.

51 Ego 'impendi pro' uobis ut me 'caperent', et inter uos et ubique pergebam causa uestra in multis periculis etiam usque ad exteras partes, ubi nemo ultra erat et ubi numquam aliquis peruenerat qui baptizaret aut clericos ordinaret aut populum consummaret, donante Domino diligenter et libentissime pro salute uestra omnia generaui. 52 Interim praemia dabam regibus praeter quod dabam mercedem filiis ipsorum qui mecum ambulant, et nihilominus comprehenderunt me cum comitibus meis et illa die auidissime cupiebant interficere me, sed tempus nondum uenerat et omnia quaecumque nobiscum inuenerunt rapuerunt illud et me ipsum ferro uinxerunt et quartodecimo die absoluit me Dominus de potestate eorum et quicquid nostrum fuit redditum est nobis propter Deum et 'necessarios amicos' quos ante praeuidimus. 53 Uos autem experti estis quantum ego erogaui illis qui iudicabant 'per omnes regiones' quos ego frequentius uisitabam. Censeo enim non minimum quam pretium quindecim hominum distribui illis, ita ut me 'fruamini' et ego 'uobis' semper 'fruar' in Deum. Non me paenitet nec satis est mihi: adhuc 'impendo et superimpendam'; potens est Dominus ut det mihi postmodum ut meipsum 'impendar pro animabus uestris'.
54 Ecce 'testem Deum inuoco in animam meam quia non mentior': neque ut sit 'occasio adulationis' uel 'auaritiae' scripserim uobis neque ut honorem spero ab aliquo uestro; sufficit enim honor qui nondum uidetur sed corde creditur; 'fidelis' autem 'qui promisit: numquam mentitur'.

51 In a áit sin, chaith mé airgead chun bhur leasa ionas go nglacfaí liom; chuaigh mé amach in bhur measc agus chuir mé mé féin i gcontúirt go minic achan áit, fiú ins na ceantair ab iargúlta, áiteanna nach raibh cónaí ar aon duine nó nar tháinig aon duine riamh le daoine a bhaisteadh, cléirigh a oirniú nó daoine a chóineartú. Ba é tíolacadh an Tiarna dom as siocair go ndearna mé gach rud daoibhse le cúram agus le díograis ar mhaithe le bhur slánú.
52 Idir amanna thugainn bronntanais do na ríthe seachas tuarastal a íoc lena gclannmhac a bhíonn ag taisteal i mo chuideachta. Mar sin féin uair amháin, d'fhuadaigh siad mé féin is mo chompánaigh agus bhí siad go fiochmhar ag brath mé a mharú an lá sin. Ach ní raibh uair na cinniúna ann. D'imigh siad le hachan rud a bhfuair siad a lámha air agus chuir siad i slabhraí mé. Ceithre lá déag ina dhiaidh sin thárrtháil an Tiarna mé óna gcrúba agus tugadh ar ais dúinn ár gcuid giúirléidí uilig trí thoil an Tiarna agus na ndlúthchairde a bhí againn roimhe seo.
53 Tá a fhios agaibh fosta an méid a dhíol mé leis na breithiúna ins na ceantair ar fad ar ghnách liom cuairt a thabhairt orthu go mion minic. Caithfidh sé gur dháil mé ar a laghad luach cúigear fear déag ina measc ionas go mbainfeadh sibhse taitneamh as mo chomhluadar agus go mbainfinnse taitneamh asaibh i nDia. Níl aiféala orm faoi seo nó ní leor liom é. Tá mé ag caitheamh go fóill agus caithfidh mé a thuilleadh. Tá sé ar chumas an Tiarna a thabhairt dom níos moille go gcaithfinn mé féin ar son bhur n-anama.
54 Amharc, iarraim ar Dhia mar fhianaise m'anama nach bhfuil mé ag inse bréige; nach bhfuil mé ag scríobh chugat le plámás nó le saint chun airgid, nó as siocair go bhfuil mé ag súil le hómós ó dhuine ar bith agaibh. Is leor an t-ómós nach bhfeictear go fóill ach atá le mothú sa chroí. Is dílis an té a gheall, ní insíonn sé bréag in am ar bith.

[55] I see that even in this world I have been exalted beyond measure by the Lord. Now I was neither worthy of this nor a likely choice for the privilege.

I know perfectly well that poverty and misfortune suit me better than riches and pleasure. Christ the Lord, himself, was poor for our sakes, and I am myself in dire straits. Even if I wished for it I have no wealth; nor do I pass judgement on myself in this matter, for I daily expect to be murdered or robbed or reduced to slavery in one way or another. Not that I fear any of these things. Because of his promises I leave myself in the hands of almighty God who rules everywhere. As the prophet says: *Cast your care upon God, and He will sustain you.*

Prayer for perseverance

[56] I now entrust my soul to God, who is most faithful and for whom I am an ambassador in my humble station. For God has no favourites and he chose me for this office to become one of his ministers, even if among the least of them [57] What return can I make to him for all his goodness to me? What can I say or what can I promise to my Lord since any ability I have comes from him? Suffice it for him to look into my heart and mind; for I am ready and indeed greatly desire it that he should give me his cup to drink, as he gave it to others who loved him. [58] My only prayer to God is that it may never happen that I should lose his people which he won for himself at the end of the earth. I ask God for perseverance, to grant that I remain a faithful witness to him for his own sake until my passing from this life.

⁵⁵ Sed uideo iam 'in praesenti saeculo' me supra modum exaltatum a Domino, et non eram dignus neque talis ut hoc mihi praestaret, dum scio certissime quod mihi melius conuenit paupertas et calamitas quam diuitiae et diliciae, sed et 'Xpistus Dominus pauper' fuit 'pro nobis', ego uero miser et infelix etsi opes uoluero iam non habeo, 'neque me ipsum iudico', quia cotidie spero aut internicionem aut circumueniri aut redigi in seruitutem siue occasio cuiuslibet, 'sed nihil horum uereor' propter promissa caelorum, quia iactaui meipsum in manus Dei omnipotentis, qui ubique dominatur. Sicut propheta dicit, 'Iacta cogitatum tuum in Deum, et ipse te enutriet'. ⁵⁶ Ecce nunc 'commendo animam meam fidelissimo Deo' meo, 'pro quo legationem fungor' in ignobilitate mea, sed quia 'personam non accipit' et eligit me ad hoc officium ut 'unus' essem 'de suis minimis' minister. ⁵⁷ Unde autem 'retribuam illi pro omnibus quae retribuit mihi'. Sed quid dicam uel quid promittam Domino meo, quia nihil ualeo nisi ipse mihi dederit? Sed 'scrutatur corda et renes' quia satis et nimis cupio et 'paratus eram' ut donaret mihi 'bibere calicem' eius, sicut indulsit et ceteris amantibus se. ⁵⁸ Quapropter non contingat mihi a Deo meo ut numquam amittam 'plebem' suam 'quam adquisiuit' in ultimis terrae. Oro Deum ut det mihi perseuerantiam et dignetur ut reddam illi testem fidelem usque ad transitum meum propter Deum meum,

⁵⁵ Tchím ar an saol seo go bhfuil moladh as cuimse tugtha ag an Tiarna dom. Anois ní raibh sé seo tuillte agam agus ní mé an sórt duine a bheadh ag súil lena leithéid. Tá a fhios agam go fiormhaith gur mó a oireann bochtaineacht agus mí-ádh dom ná saibhreas agus só. Bhí Críost an Tiarna é féin bocht ar ár son agus tá mé féin in umar na haimiléise. Fiú dá mba mhian liom é, níl saibhreas agam; nó ní thugaim breithiúnas orm féin sa chás seo, nó níl lá nach mbím ag brath go ndéanfar mé a dhúnmharú, nó go ndéanfar rudaí a ghoid uaim nó sclábhaí a dhéanamh díom nó go dtarlóidh mí-ádh éigin dom. Ní hé go bhfuil eagla orm roimh na rudaí seo. De bharr a ghealltanais fágaim mé féin i lámha Dé uilechumhachtaigh a rialaíonn gach áit. Mar a deir an fáidh: *Cuir do chúram faoi choimirce Dé agus cothóidh sé thú.*
⁵⁶ Cuirim cúram m'anama anois i nDia atá fíordhílis agus a bhfuil mé i mo thoscaire dó dá dhonacht mé. De bhrí go bhfuil sé gan fabhar do dhuine seachas a chéile thogh sé mise don oifig seo le bheith i mo mhinistir aige, as an chuid is lú acu. ⁵⁷ Caidé an t-aisíoc a thig liom a dhéanamh leis as ucht a chinéaltais dom? Caidé a thig liom a rá nó a gheallstan don Tiarna mar gur uaidh a tháinig gach aon chumas atá ionam? Is leor a rá go dtig leis mo chroí agus m'intinn a scrúdú; mar tá mé réidh agus tá fonn mór orm go dtabharfaidh sé a chailís dom le hól mar a thug sé do dhaoine eile a raibh grá acu dó. ⁵⁸ Mar sin nár lige mo Dhia dom go gcaillfinn a choíche an pobal a mheall sé chuige féin ag críocha an domhain. Iarraim buansheasmhacht ar Dhia a dheonú dom go mbeidh mé i mo fhinné dílis dó ar a shon féin go dtí go dtrasnaím ón saol seo.

[59] If I ever did anything worth doing for my God, whom I love, I beg of him the grace to shed my blood while still with those who are also exiles and captives on his account. Though I should be denied a grave, though my corpse should be utterly torn to pieces and scattered to dogs and wild animals, though the birds of the air should devour it; I would be fully confident in this event that I had saved both body and soul. For on that day we will undoubtedly rise in the brightness of the sun, that is, in the glory of Christ Jesus our Redeemer, as sons of the living God, joint heirs with Christ and made in his image. From him and through him and for him we will reign. [60] This sun which we see rises daily at his command for our benefit, but will never reign, nor will its brilliance endure. Those who worship it will be severely punished. We, on the other hand, believe in and worship Christ the true sun who will never perish, nor will anyone who does his will. He will remain for ever as Christ remains for ever, who reigns with God the Father Almighty and the Holy Spirit before time began and now and for all eternity. Amen.

Briefly

Look, [61] I wish to explain briefly the words of my confession again and again. Before God and his holy angels I solemnly and gladly swear that I had never any motive other than the Gospel and its promises to go back to that nation from which previously I had only barely escaped.

A final request

[62] A request of those who believe and revere God. If any of you see fit to examine or to obtain this document, which has been written in Ireland by Patrick an uneducated sinner, do not attribute to me in my ignorance the little I achieved or pointed out that pleased God. Let your conclusion and the general opinion rather be the real truth, that my success was the gift of God.

This is my confession before I die.

⁵⁹ et si aliquid boni umquam imitatus sum propter Deum meum, quem diligo, peto illi det mihi ut cum illis proselitis et captiuis pro nomine suo effundam sanguinem meum, etsi ipsam etiam caream sepulturam aut miserissime cadauer per singula membra diuidatur canibus aut bestiis asperis aut 'uolucres caeli comederent illud'. Certissime reor, si mihi hoc incurrisset, lucratus sum animam cum corpore meo, quia 'sine ulla dubitatione' in die illa 'resurgemus' in claritate solis, hoc est, 'in gloria' Xpisti Iesu redemptoris nostri, quasi 'filii Dei' uiui et 'coheredes Xpisti' et 'conformes futuri imaginis ipsius'; quoniam 'ex ipso et per ipsum et in ipso' regnaturi sumus. ⁶⁰ Nam sol iste quem uidemus ipso iubente propter nos cotidie oritur, sed numquam regnabit neque permanebit splendor eius, sed et omnes qui adorant eum in poenam miseri male deuenient; nos autem qui credimus et adoramus solem uerum Xpistum, qui numquam interibit neque 'qui fecerit uoluntatem' ipsius, sed 'manebit in aeternum quomodo et Xpistus manet in aeternum', qui regnat cum Deo Patre Omnipotente et cum Spiritu Sancto ante saecula et nunc et per omnia saecula saeculorum. Amen. ⁶¹ Ecce iterum iterumque breuiter exponam uerba Confessionis meae. 'Testificor' in ueritate et in 'exultatione cordis coram Deo et sanctis angelis eius' quia numquam habui aliquam occasionem praeter euangelium et promissa illius ut umquam redirem ad gentem illam unde prius uix euaseram. ⁶² Sed precor credentibus et timentibus Deum, quicumque dignatus fuerit inspicere uel recipere hanc scripturam quam Patricius peccator indoctus scilicet Hiberione conscripsit, ut nemo umquam dicat quod mea ignorantia si aliquid pusillum egi uel demonstrauerim secundum Dei placitum, sed arbitramini et uerissime credatur quod 'donum Dei' fuisset. Et haec est Confessio mea antequam moriar.

⁵⁹ Má éirigh liom riamh aon rud maith arbh fhiú dada é a dhéanamh do mo Dhia a bhfuil grá agam dó, impím air a dheonú dom m' fhuil a dhoirteadh agus mé go fóill leo seo atá ina mbraighdeanaigh ar a shon. Fiú mura mbeadh uaigh le fáil agam, fiú dá mbeadh mo chorp iomlán stróicthe ina ghiotaí agus caite chuig madaí agus ainmhithe fiáine, fiú dá n-alpfadh éanlaith an aeir é, dá dtarlódh sin; tá mé lánchinnte go mbeinn slán idir anam agus chorp. Mar an lá sin aiséireoimid gan amhras i ngile na gréine, 'sé sin, i nglóir Íosa Críost ár Slánaitheoir, mar mhic Dhia na beatha, mar chomhoidhrí Chríost agus mar mhacasamhail a dheilbhe; nó is uaidh agus tríd agus ann atáimid le bheith i réim. ⁶⁰ Éiríonn an ghrian seo a tchímid achan lá ar ordú uaidhsean ar ár son, ach ní thiocfaidh sí i réim a choíche nó ní mhairfidh a gile. Cuirfear pionós mór ar na daoine a adhraíonn í. Ar an láimh eile adhraímidne Críost an fhíorghrian nach n-éagann choíche, nó aon duine eile a dhéanann a thoil. Mairfidh sé go deo mar a mhairfidh Críost go deo, a rialaíonn le Dia an tAthair uilechumhachtach agus an Spiorad Naomh, roimh na haoiseanna agus anois agus le saol na saol. Amen. ⁶¹ Amharc, is mian liom gearrmhíniú a dhéanamh ar fhocail m'fhaoistine arís agus arís eile. Os comhair Dé agus a aingeal naofa tugaim móid go sollúnta agus le háthas nach raibh aon chúis riamh agam ach amháin an Soiscéal agus a ghealltanais, a dhul ar ais go dtí an cine gurb ar éigean ar éirigh liom éalú uathu roimhe sin. ⁶² Seo achainí dóibh siúd a chreideann agus a thugann urraim do Dhia. Má bhíonn an deis ag aon duine agaibh an cháipéis seo a fháil nó a scrúdú, an cháipéis seo a scríobh Pádraig, peacach gan oiliúint in Éirinn, ná cuir síos domsa, i m'aineolaí agus mar atá mé, an beagán a bhain mé amach nó a thug mé chun solais a thug sásamh do Dhia. Tugaigí bhur mbreithiúnas agus bíodh an tuairim is fírinní agaibh gur tíolacadh ó Dhia a bhí ann. Sin í m' fhaoistin sula n-éagaim.

EPISTOLA AD MILITES COROTICI/LITIR CHUIG SAIGHDIÚIRÍ COROTICUS

Patrick's right to protest

1 I, Patrick, a sinner and untaught, established in Ireland, declare myself to be a bishop. I believe most firmly that what I am I have received from God. That is why I live among uncivilised people, a stranger and exile for the love of God. He is my witness that this is so. Not that I have usually wanted to speak out in such a severe harsh way. But I am compelled by concern for God. The truth of Christ has aroused me, out of love for my neighbours and children, for whom I have given up homeland and family, and my own life even to death. If I am worthy, I live only for God to teach the heathens, even though some despise me.

2 With my own hand I have written down these words. I composed them to be related and passed on, in order that they may be sent to the soldiers of Coroticus. I do not say to my fellow-citizens or to the fellow-citizens of the holy Romans but to the fellow-citizens of the devils, because of their evil actions. In their hostile behaviour they live in death, these allies of the Scoto-Irish, Picts and apostates. Dripping with blood they wallow in the slaughter of innocent Christians, whom I personally brought into the life of the baptised and confirmed in Christ.

3 The newly-baptised in their white garments had just been anointed with chrism. It was still giving forth its scent on their foreheads when they were cruelly and brutally murdered, put to the sword by these men I have already mentioned. The next day I sent a letter with a holy presbyter in the company of clerics, a man I had taught from his childhood. We wanted something saved from the plunder, some of the baptised prisoners spared. They made fun of them.

¹ Patricius peccator indoctus scilicet Hiberione constitutus episcopum me esse fateor. Certissime reor a Deo 'accepi id quod sum'. Inter barbaras itaque gentes habito proselitus et profuga ob amorem Dei; testis est ille si ita est. Non quod optabam tam dure et tam aspere aliquid ex ore meo effundere, sed cogor zelo Dei et ueritas Xpisti excitauit, pro dilectione proximorum atque filiorum, pro quibus 'tradidi' patriam et parentes et 'animam meam usque ad mortem'. Si dignus sum uiuo Deo meo docere gentes etsi contempnor aliquibus. ² Manu mea scripsi atque condidi uerba ista danda et tradenda militibus mittenda Corotici, non dico ciuibus meis neque ciuibus sanctorum Romanorum sed ciuibus daemoniorum ob mala opera ipsorum. Ritu hostili in morte uiuunt, socii Scottorum atque Pictorum apostatarumque, sanguilentos sanguinare de sanguine innocentium Xpistianorum, 'quos' ego innumerum numerum Deo 'genui' atque 'in Xpisto' confirmaui. ³ Postera die qua crismati neophyti in ueste candida – flagrabat in fronte ipsorum dum crudeliter trucidati atque mactati gladio supradictis – misi epistolam cum sancto presbytero quem ego ex infantia docui cum clericis ut nobis aliquid indulgerent de praeda uel de captiuis baptizatis quos ceperunt: cachinnos fecerunt de illis.

¹ Mise Pádraig, peacach gan oiliúint, i mo chónaí in Éirinn, fógraím gur easpag mé. Creidim go diongbháilte gur ó Dhia a fuair mé a mbaineann liom. Sin an fáth a bhfuil mé i mo chónaí i measc dream míshibhialta, i mo choimhthíoch agus i mo dheoraí ar son Dé. Is é m'fhianaise gur seo mar atá. Ní hé gur mhaith liom de ghnáth labhairt amach ar dhóigh ghéar, shearbh. Ach sáraíonn díograis do Dhia mé agus ghríosaigh fírinne Chríost mé de barr ghrá comharsan agus clainne ar thug mé suas ar a son mo bhaile dúchais agus mo theaghlach agus mo shaol féin go bás. Má tá sé tuillte agam, mairim do Dhia amháin leis na págánaigh a theagasc cé gur beag ar roinnt daoine mé.
² Is le mo láimh féin atá na focail seo scríofa síos. Chum mé iad lena n-aithris agus a gcur ar aghaidh ionas go seolfar chuig saighdiúirí Coroticus iad. Ní deirim chuig mo chomhshaoránaigh nó chuig comhshaoránaigh na Rómhánach naofa ach chuig comhshaoránaigh na ndiabhal de bharr a ndrochghníomhartha. Maireann siad sa bhás dála naimhde, i gcomhar leis na Scotaigh agus na Cruithnigh agus leo siúd a shéan an creideamh. Le fuil ar a lámha agus fuil ar sileadh leo, glacann siad páirt i slad ar Chríostaithe neamhurchóideacha a ghin mé ina sluaite do Dhia agus a chóineartaigh mé i gCríost.
³ Ní raibh an lucht nua-bhaiste ach i ndiaidh a n-ungtha le criosma agus iad in éadaí geala. Bhí an cumhrán go fóill ar a n-éadan nuair a dúnmharaíodh go danartha agus go brúidiúil iad leis an chlaíomh ag an dream thuasluaite. Lá arna mhárach chuir mé litir le cruifear naofa, a d'oil mé ó bhí sé ina naíonán, agus cléirigh ina chuideachta. Ba mhian linn go dtabharfaidís cuid den slad ar ais dúinn, cuid de na príosúnaigh bhaiste a thóg siad. Rinne siad ábhar gáire dóibh.

Sins must be punished

⁴ Consequently, I do not know for whom I am to grieve the more; whether for those who were killed, for those whom they captured, or those whom the devil has deeply ensnared. Together with him they will be slaves of hell in everlasting punishment. For everyone who commits sin is a slave and is called a child of the devil. ⁵ Therefore, let every God-fearing person know that they are estranged from me and from Christ my God, whose ambassador I am. They are murderers of father and of brother, fierce wolves devouring the people of the Lord as they would a loaf of bread. As Scripture says: *Lord, the wicked have destroyed your law,* your law which but recently he had in his kindness successfully planted in Ireland, and which was taught by God's favour.

⁶ I am no usurper. My lot is with those whom he called and predestined to preach the Gospel among bitter persecutions even to the ends of the earth. I do this even though the enemy shows his jealousy through the tyranny of Coroticus, a man without respect either for God or for his priests whom he chose and graciously granted the highest form of supreme divine power, that those whom they bind on earth should be bound also in heaven.

⁷ So, I make these special requests of you, devout and humble-hearted men. It is not permitted to court the favour of such people, to take food or drink with them, or even to accept their alms. They must first make reparation to God through rigorous penance and in floods of tears. They must have freed the servants of God and baptised handmaids of Christ, for whom he died and was crucified.

⁸ The Most High rejects the gifts of the wicked. Offering sacrifice from the property of the poor is just as evil as slaughtering a son in the presence of his father. *The riches,* says Scripture, *which he gathered unjustly shall be vomited up from his belly; the angel of death drags him away; with the fury of dragons he shall be beaten; the viper's tongue shall slay him; unquenchable fire shall devour him.*

4 Idcirco nescio quid magis lugeam: an qui interfecti uel quos ceperunt uel quos grauiter zabulus inlaqueauit. Perenni poena gehennam pariter cum ipso mancipabunt quia utique 'qui facit peccatum seruus est' et 'filius zabuli' nuncupatur. 5 Quapropter resciat omnis homo timens Deum quod a me alieni sunt et a Xpisto Deo meo 'pro quo legationem fungor', patricida, fratricida, 'lupi rapaces deuorantes plebem Domini ut cibum panis', sicut ait 'Iniqui dissipauerunt legem tuam, Domine', quam in supremis temporibus Hiberione optime benigne plantauerat atque instructa erat fauente Deo. 6 Non usurpo. Partem habeo cum his 'quos aduocauit et praedestinauit' evangelium praedicare in persecutionibus non paruis 'usque ad extremum terrae', etsi inuidet inimicus per tyrannidem Coroticum, qui Deum non ueretur nec sacerdotes ipsius, quos elegit et indulsit illis summam diuinam sublimam potestatem, 'quos ligarent super terram ligatos esse et in caelis'. 7 Unde ergo quaeso plurimum 'sancti et humiles corde' adulari talibus non licet 'nec cibum' nec potum 'sumere' cum ipsis nec elemosinas ipsorum recipi debeat donec crudeliter paenitentiam effusis lacrimis satis Deo faciant et liberent seruos Dei et ancillas Xpisti baptizatas, pro quibus mortuus est et crucifixus. 8 'Dona iniquorum reprobat Altissimus.' 'Qui offert sacrificium ex substantia pauperum quasi qui uictimat filium in conspectu patris sui.' 'Diuitias' inquit 'quas congregauit iniuste euomentur de uentre eius, trahit illum angelus mortis, ira draconum mulcabitur, interficiet illum lingua colubris, comedit autem eum ignis inextinguibilis'

4 Ar an ábhar sin níl a fhios agam cé acu is mó is ábhar buartha dom, na daoine a maraíodh, iadsan a gabhadh, nó iad ar rug an diabhal go dian orthu. Beidh siad ina sclábhaithe ifrinn lena bpianta síoraí maraon leis-sean. Mar gach duine a dhéanann peaca is sclábhaí é agus bhéarfar mac an diabhail air. 5 Dá bhrí sin bíodh a fhios ag gach duine ar eagal leis Dia go bhfuil siad in easaontas liomsa agus le Críost mo Dhia a bhfuil mé i mo thoscaire ar a shon. Is dúnmharfóirí athar agus bráthar iad, mic tíre chraosacha a alpann pobal Dé mar a bheadh arán ann. Mar a deir an Scrioptúr: *A Thiarna, tá do dhlí scriosta ag lucht an oilc*, dlí a bhí bunaithe aige go fiormhaith agus go cineálta in Éirinn ar na mallaibh agus a múineadh le grásta Dé.

6 Ní forlámhaí ar bith mé. Tá mé i bpáirt leo sin ar ghlaoigh sé orthu agus ar shocraigh sé roimh ré an Soiscéal a chraobhscaoileadh ina measc i lár géarleanúintí nár bheag, fiú go críocha an domhain. Tá sé seo ar siúl agam cé go gcaitheann an namhaid drochshúil linn trí ansmacht Coroticus, fear nach bhfuil urraim aige do Dhia nó do na sagairt atá tofa aige agus ar bhronn sé an chumhacht dhiaga ab airde agus ab uaisle orthu, ionas go mbeadh ceangal ar neamh orthu siúd ar cuireadh ceangal orthu ar talamh.

7 Dá bhrí sin, impím go dúthrachtach oraibhse atá naofa agus umhal ó chroí. Níl sé ceadaithe a leithéidí seo a mholadh nó bia nó deoch a ghlacadh leo nó fiú déirc a ghlacadh uathu. Caithfidh siad ar dtús cúiteamh a dhéanamh le Dia trí aithrí dhian agus sileadh na ndeor. Caithfidh siad searbhóntaí Dé agus bansheirbhísigh bhaiste Chríost a shaoradh, Críost a fuair bás agus a céasadh ar chrois ar a son.

8 Diúltaíonn an té is airde tabhartais na n-urchóideach. Is ionann ofráil íobairte ó mhaoin na mbocht le marú mic i láthair an athar. Mar a deir an Scrioptúr: *An mhaoin a chruinnigh sé go héagórach caithfear amach as a bholg é; tarraingíonn aingeal an bháis ar shiúl é; le fíoch na ndragún buailfear é; maróidh teanga na nathrach nimhe é; alpfaidh tine dhomhúchta é.*

Therefore: *Woe to those who fill themselves with what is not their own.*
And again: *What does it profit a man that he should gain the whole world
and suffer the loss of his own soul?* [9] It would be tedious to discuss or to
mention every single text, to gather proofs from the whole Law
relating to such greed. Avarice is a deadly sin. *You shall not covet your
neighbour's goods. You shall not kill.* A murderer cannot be with Christ.
He who hates his brother is to be considered a murderer. *He who does
not love his brother remains in death.* How much more guilty is he who
has stained his hands with the blood of the children of God whom he
has recently gathered at the ends of the earth through the preaching
of my insignificant self?

Patrick isolated

[10] Surely it was not without reference to God or for merely human
purposes that I came to Ireland? Who compelled me? I am bound by
the Spirit not to see any of my relatives. Surely it is not from myself
that my ministry of mercy to that people derives, that people who
once kidnapped me and made away with the men and women
servants of my father's house? I was born free in worldly status. My
father was a decurion. But I sold my noble rank without shame or
regret for the benefit of others. Thus I am a servant in Christ to a far-
off nation on account of the indescribable glory of eternal life which
is in Christ Jesus our Lord.

[11] And if my own people do not recognise me, *a prophet has no honour
in his own country.* Perhaps we do not belong to the same fold and do
not have the same God as Father. As he says: *He who is not with me is
against me, and he who does not gather with me scatters.* There is no
agreement: *One man pulls down and another builds up.* I do not seek
what is my own. It is not my virtue but God who put this concern
into my heart that I should become one of the huntsmen or
fishermen whom God once foretold would come in the last days.

ideoque 'Uae qui replent se quae non sunt sua', uel 'Quid prodest homini ut totum mundum lucretur et animae suae detrimentum patiatur?' [9] Longum est per singula discutere uel insinuare, per totam legem carpere testimonia de tali cupiditate. Auaritia mortale crimen. 'Non concupisces rem proximi tui. Non occides.' Homicida non potest esse cum Xpisto. 'Qui odit fratrem suum homicida' adscribitur uel 'Qui non diligit fratrem suum in morte manet'. Quanto magis reus est qui manus suas coinquinauit in sanguine filiorum Dei, quos nuper 'adquisiuit' in ultimis terrae per exhortationem paruitatis nostrae?

[10] Numquid sine Deo uel 'secundum carnem' Hiberione ueni? Quis me compulit? 'Alligatus' sum 'Spiritu' ut non uideam aliquem 'de cognatione mea'. Numquid a me piam misericordiam quod ago erga gentem illam qui me aliquando ceperunt et deuastauerunt seruos et ancillas domus patris mei? Ingenuus fui 'secundum carnem'; decurione patre nascor. Uendidi enim nobilitatem meam – non erubesco neque me paenitet – pro utilitate aliorum; denique seruus sum in Xpisto genti exterae ob gloriam ineffabilem 'perennis uitae quae est in Xpisto Iesu Domino nostro'. [11] Et si mei me non cognoscunt 'propheta in patria sua honorem non habet'. Forte non sumus 'ex uno ouili' neque 'unum Deum patrem' habemus, sicut ait 'Qui non est mecum contra me est et qui non congregat mecum spargit'. Non conuenit: 'Unus destruit, alter aedificat.' 'Non quaero quae mea sunt.' Non mea gratia sed Deus 'qui dedit hanc sollicitudinem in corde meo' ut unus essem de 'uenatoribus siue piscatoribus' quos olim Deus 'in nouissimis diebus' ante praenuntiauit.

Mar sin: *Is mairg dóibh sin a líonann iad féin le nithe nach leo.* Agus arís: *Caidé an mhaith do dhuine an domhan mór a ghnóthú agus a anam féin a ligint le fán?*

[9] Bheadh sé leadránach achan téacs a phlé nó a lua agus cruthúnas ón dlí go léir a lorg i dtaobh an sórt sin sainte. *Is coir mharfach í an tsaint. Ná santaigh cuid do chomharsan. Ná déan marú.* Ní féidir le dúnmharfóir a bheith le Críost. An té a bhfuil fuath aige ar a bhráthair is meas dúnmharfóra a bheas air. *An té nach bhfuil grá aige dá bhráthair fanann sé sa bhás.* Nach ciontaí go mór atá an té a d'fhág smál ar a lámha le fuil chlann Dé, an chlann a chruinnigh sé le chéile ar na mallaibh ag críocha an domhain trí mo spreagadh-sa dá laghad mé?

[10] An é gur tháinig mé go hÉirinn gan Dia a bheith liom nó ar chúrsaí saolta? Cé a chuir iallach orm? Tá crosta ag an Spiorad orm duine ar bith de mo ghaolta a fheiceáil. Cinnte ní uaim féin a thagann ministreacht na trócaire chuig an phobal sin a ghabh mé uair amháin agus a rinne creach de na seirbhísigh a bhí i dteach m'athar idir fhir agus mhná. Rugadh i mo shaoránach mé de réir na colla. Ba decurion m'athair. Dhíol mé m'uaisleacht ar mhaithe le daoine eile, rud nach gcuireann náire nó aiféala orm. Mar sin is searbhónta mé i gCríost go náisiún i bhfad i gcéin ar son ghlóir do-inste na beatha síoraí atá i gCríost Íosa ár dTiarna

[11] Agus mura n-aithníonn mo mhuintir féin mé, *ní fhaigheann fáidh onóir ina thír dhúchais.* B'fhéidir nach bhfuil baint againn leis an tréad céanna agus nach bhfuil an Dia céanna againn mar athair? Mar a deir sé: *An té nach bhfuil liom tá sé i m'aghaidh agus an té nach gcruinníonn liom scaipeann sé.* Níltear ar aon intinn. *Leagann duine amháin agus tógann duine eile.* Níl mé ag lorg mo choda féin. Ní domsa a bhuíochas ach do Dhia a chuir an cúram seo i mo chroí gur cheart dom a bheith ar dhuine de na sealgairí nó de na hiascairí a ndearn a Dia tairngreacht fúthu fadó go dtiocfaidís ins na laethanta deireanacha.

Murder for money

12 I am looked on with hate. What am I to do, Lord? I am greatly despised. Look, your sheep are torn to pieces around me and plundered by that miserable band of robbers at the bidding of the evil-minded Coroticus. Far from the love of God is the betrayer of Christians into the hands of the Scoto-Irish and the Picts. Ravenous wolves have gobbled up the flock of the Lord, which in Ireland under excellent care was really flourishing, countless sons of Scoto-Irish and the daughters of their kings having become monks and virgins for Christ. For this reason may the wrong done to the just find no pleasure with you, Lord, even as it makes its way to the depths of hell. 13 Which of the faithful would not shrink in horror from making merry or enjoying a meal with people of this sort? They have filled their houses with the spoils of dead Christians, they make their living on plunder. The wretches do not know that what they are offering as food to their friends and children is deadly poison, just as Eve did not understand that it was death she was offering her husband. So are all who do evil: by causing death they bring about their eternal punishment.

14 This is the custom of the Christians of Roman Gaul: they send holy and suitable men to the Franks and other heathens with so many thousands of shillings to ransom baptised prisoners. But you, on the contrary, murder them and sell them to a far-off nation that does not know God. You hand over the members of Christ into what could be called a brothel. What hope have you in God, or anyone who thinks like you or converses with you in words of flattery? God will judge. For it is written: *Not only they who do evil, but also they who approve of them, shall be condemned.*

[12] Inuidetur mihi. Quid faciam, Domine? Ualde despicior. Ecce oues tuae circa me laniantur atque depraedantur et supradictis latrunculis iubente Corotico hostili mente. Longe est a caritate Dei traditor Xpistianorum in manus Scottorum atque Pictorum. 'Lupi rapaces' deglutierunt gregem Domini, qui utique Hiberione cum summa diligentia optime crescebat, et filii Scottorum et filiae regulorum monachi et uirgines Xpisti enumerare nequeo. Quam ob rem 'iniuria iustorum non te placeat'; etiam 'usque ad inferos non placebit'. [13] Quis sanctorum non horreat iocundare uel conuiuium fruere cum talibus? De spoliis defunctorum Xpistianorum repleuerunt domos suas, de rapinis uiuunt. Nesciunt miseri uenenum letale cibum porrigunt ad amicos et filios suos, sicut Eua non intellexit quod utique mortem tradidit uiro suo. Sic sunt omnes qui male agunt: 'mortem' perennem poenam 'operantur'.

[14] Consuetudo Romanorum Gallorum Xpistianorum: mittunt uiros sanctos idoneos ad Francos et ceteras gentes cum tot milia solidorum ad redimendos captiuos baptizatos. Tu potius interficis et uendis illos genti exterae ignoranti Deum; quasi in lupanar tradis 'membra Xpisti'. Qualem spem habes in Deum uel qui te consentit aut qui te communicat uerbis adulationis? Deus iudicabit. Scriptum est enim 'Non solum facientes mala sed etiam consentientes damnandi sunt.'

[12] Tá fuath ag daoine orm. Caidé atá le déanamh agam a Thiarna? Tá fíor-dhrochmheas orm. Amharc, tá do chuid caorach stróicthe ina bpíosaí thart orm agus slad déanta ag na gadaithe thuasluaite ar ordú ó Coroticus na drochaigne. Is fada ó ghrá Dé fealltóir na gCríostaithe isteach i lámha na Scotach agus na gCruithneach. D'alp mic tíre chraosacha tréad an Tiarna a bhí faoi bhláth in Éirinn de bharr cúraim fhíormhaith. Níl áireamh agam ar chlannmhac na Scotach agus ar iníonacha ríthe a bhí ina manaigh agus ina maighdeana le Críost. Ar an ábhar sin ná bain sásamh as an éagóir a rinneadh ar na fíréin, a Thiarna, ní bhainfear sásamh as ar a bhealach dó go híochtar ifrinn fiú. [13] Cé acu de na fíréin nár ghráin leo a bheith ag spraoi nó ag baint sult as fleá lena leithéidí? Líon siad a dtithe le creach na gCríostaithe marbha: is ar slad a bhaineann siad amach a mbeatha. Níl a fhios ag na hainniseoirí gur nimh mharfach atá siad a ofráil mar bhia dá gcairde agus dá gclann, díreach mar nár thuig Éabha gurbh é an bás a bhí a ofráil aici dá fear céile. Mar sin atá na daoine go léir a dhéanann an t-olc: saothraíonn siad an bás síoraí mar phionós.

[14] Is nós é seo ag Críostaithe na Gaille Rómhánaí: cuireann siad fir naofa oiriúnacha chun na bhFrancach agus na bpágánach eile leis na mílte scilling, le príosúnaigh bhaiste a fhuascailt. Ach déanann tusa a mhalairt, maraíonn tú agus díolann tú iad le náisiúin i bhfad i gcéin nach eol dóibh Dia, tugann tú baill Chríost suas d'áit a bhféadfaí teach striapachais a thabhairt air. Caidé an dóchas atá agat i nDia nó ag duine ar bith atá ar aon intinn leat nó a bhíonn ag tabhairt béil bháin duit? Bhéarfaidh Dia breithiúnas, nó tá sé scríofa: *Ní amháin na daoine a dhéanann an t-olc a dhaorfar, ach iadsan a aontaíonn leo chomh maith.*

Grief and consolation

15 I do not know what more I can say, or speak, about the departed of the children of God whom the sword struck down all too harshly. For it is written: *Weep with those who weep.* And elsewhere: *If one member suffers, let all the members suffer with it.* Therefore, the Church mourns and laments her sons and daughters, not yet slain by the sword, but who are in exile, having been carried away into distant lands where serious and shameless sin openly abounds. Free men are sold there as slaves, Christians are reduced to slavery, and worst of all, given over to the most worthless and the vilest apostates and Picts.

16 Therefore, I will cry aloud in sorrow and grief: fairest and most dearly beloved brothers and sons, whom I begot in Christ in countless members, what can I do for you? I am unworthy to be helping either God or people. The wickedness of the wicked has prevailed over us. We have been treated like aliens. Perhaps they do not believe that we have received one and the same baptism or that we have one and the same God as Father. They think it a matter of contempt that we are Irish. Scripture says: *Have you not one God? Why have you abandoned each one of you his neighbour?*

17 Therefore, I lament for you, I lament, my dearly beloved. But again, I rejoice in my heart. I have not laboured for nothing: my travels have not been in vain. Again if this outrage, so dreadful, so unspeakable, had to happen, then God be thanked that you have left this world for Paradise as baptised Christians. I can see you: You have begun to journey where night will be no more, nor mourning nor death. But you will leap like calves freed from the tether: you will trample on the wicked and they will be like ashes under your feet.

[15] Nescio 'quid dicam' uel 'quid loquar' amplius de defunctis filiorum Dei, quos gladius supra modum dure tetigit. Scriptum est enim 'Flete cum flentibus' et iterum 'Si dolet unum membrum condoleant omnia membra'. Quapropter ecclesia 'plorat et plangit filios' et filias 'suas' quas adhuc gladius nondum interfecit, sed prolongati et exportati in longa terrarum, ubi 'peccatum' manifeste grauiter impudenter 'abundat', ibi uenundati ingenui homines, Xpistiani in seruitute redacti sunt, praesertim indignissimorum pessimorum apostatarumque Pictorum.

[16] Idcirco cum tristitia et maerore uociferabo: O speciosissimi atque amantissimi fratres et filii 'quos in Christo genui' enumerare nequeo, quid faciam uobis? Non sum dignus Deo neque hominibus subuenire. 'Praeualuit iniquitas iniquorum super nos.' Quasi 'extranei facti sumus'. Forte non credunt 'unum baptismum' percepimus uel 'unum Deum patrem' habemus. Indignum est illis Hiberionaci sumus. Sicut ait 'Nonne unum Deum habetis?' 'Quid dereliquistis unusquisque proximum suum?'

[17] Idcirco doleo pro uobis, doleo, carissimi mihi; sed iterum gaudeo intra meipsum: non gratis 'laboraui' uel peregrinatio mea 'in uacuum' non fuit. Et contigit scelus tam horrendum ineffabile, Deo gratias, creduli baptizati, de saeculo recessistis ad paradisum. Cerno uos: migrare coepistis ubi 'nox non erit' 'neque luctus neque mors amplius', 'sed exultabitis sicut uituli ex uinculis resoluti et conculcabitis iniquos et erunt cinis sub pedibus uestris'.

[15] Níl a fhios agam caidé eile a thig liom a rá nó a chur le mo chaint faoi chlann Dé atá marbh, a gearradh síos ag an chláíomh chomh cadránta sin? Nó tá sé scríofa: *Sil deora leis na daoine a shileann deora.* Agus in áit eile: *Má bhíonn duine amháin ag fulaingt, bíodh gach duine ag fulaingt leis.* Mar sin bíonn an Eaglais ag caoineadh a clannmhac agus iníonacha nár maraíodh go fóill leis an chláíomh ach atá díbeartha agus tógtha ar shiúl go tíortha i bhfad i gcéin, mar a bhfuil an peaca go fairsing agus é soiléir, tromchúiseach agus náireach. Díoladh saoránaigh ansin, rinneadh sclábhaithe de Chríostaithe, agus an rud is measa, iad i lámha na n-ainchreidmheach, an dream is urchóidí agus is suaraí ar fad, agus na gCruithneach.

[16] Dá bhrí sin glaofaidh mé os ard faoi bhrón agus faoi léan: a bhráithre agus a mhaca, an dream is breátha agus is ansa liom, a ghin mé in bhur sluaite i gCríost, caidé a thig liom a dhéanamh daoibh? Ní fiú mé a bheith ag cuidiú le Dia nó le daoine. Tá an lámh in uachtar ag danarthacht an dreama mhallaithe orainn. Glactar linn mar choimhthígh. Ní dócha go gcreideann siad gurbh é an baisteadh amháin a fuaireamar agus gurb é an Dia amháin atá mar athair againn. Is ábhar drochmheasa dóibh gur Éireannaigh muid. Mar a deir an Scrioptúr: *Nach aon Dia amháin atá agaibh? Cén fáth gur thréig sibh, gach duine agaibh, bhur gcomharsa?*

[17] Mar sin, tá mé ag caoi ar bhur son, tá mé ag caoi, a mhuintir ionmhuin. Ach arís tá áthas croí orm. Ní raibh mo shaothar in aisce agam; ní gan toradh a bhí mo chuid taistil. Má b'éigean don choir uafásach do-inste seo tarlú, gabhaim buíochas le Dia gur fhág sibh an saol seo le dul go Parthas mar Chríostaithe baiste. Is féidir liom sibh a fheiceáil. Tá bhur dtriall ar an tír nach mbeidh oíche níos mó ann, nó mairgneach nó bás. Ach léimfidh sibh mar ghamhna a saoradh ón téad: déanfaidh sibh satailt ar an dream mallaithe agus beidh siad mar luaith faoi bhur gcosa.

¹⁸ You will reign with apostles and prophets and martyrs. You will receive everlasting kingdoms. As he himself testifies, saying: *They shall come from the east and from west and sit at table with Abraham and Isaac and Jacob in the kingdom of heaven. Outside shall be the dogs and sorcerers and murderers; and: As for liars and perjurers, their lot shall be in the lake of everlasting fire.* It is not without justice that the Apostle says: *Seeing that the righteous man shall only with trouble be saved, the sinner then and the impious transgressor of the law – where will he find himself?*

The sinners must repent

¹⁹ And as for Coroticus and his criminals, rebels against Christ, where will they see themselves, men who distribute young baptised women as spoil in the service of a vile earthly kingdom which may of course disappear in a moment? Like a cloud of smoke dispersed by the wind, deceitful sinners will perish when God approaches. But good men will feast with Christ without interruption, they will judge nations and they will rule over wicked kings forever and ever. Amen.

²⁰ I testify before God and his angels that it will happen as he has indicated to me, ignorant though I may be. These are not my words which I have set out in Latin, but the words of God and of apostles and prophets: and they have never told lies. *He who believes shall be saved, but he who does not believe shall be condemned.* God has spoken.

¹⁸ Uos ergo regnabitis cum apostolis et prophetis atque martyribus. Aeterna regna capietis, sicut ipse testatur inquit 'Uenient ab oriente et occidente et recumbent cum Abraham et Isaac et Iacob in regno caelorum. Foris canes et uenefici et homicidae' et 'Mendacibus periuris pars eorum in stagnum ignis aeterni.' Non inmerito ait apostolus 'Ubi iustus uix saluus erit peccator et impius transgressor legis ubi se recognoscet?'
¹⁹ Unde enim Coroticus cum suis sceleratissimis, rebellatores Xpisti, ubi se uidebunt, qui mulierculas baptizatas praemia distribuunt ob miserum regnum temporale, quod utique in momento transeat? 'Sicut nubes uel fumus, qui utique uento dispergitur', ita 'peccatores' fraudulenti 'a facie Domini peribunt; iusti autem epulentur in magna constantia' cum Xpisto 'iudicabunt nationes et' regibus iniquis 'dominabuntur' in saecula saeculorum. Amen.
²⁰ 'Testificor coram Deo et angelis suis' quod ita erit sicut intimauit imperitiae meae. Non mea uerba sed Dei et apostolorum atque prophetarum quod ego Latinum exposui, qui numquam enim mentiti sunt. 'Qui crediderit saluus erit, qui uero non crediderit condempnabitur, Deus locutus est.'

¹⁸ Beidh sibh i réim leis na haspail, na fáithe agus na mairtírigh. Bainfidh sibh na flaithis shíoraí amach. Mar a thugann sé féin fianaise a rá: *Tiocfaidh siad anoir agus aniar agus suífidh siad ag tábla le hAbrahám agus le hÍosác agus le Iacób i ríocht na bhflaitheas. Taobh amuigh beidh na madaí, na draoithe agus na dúnmharfóirí*; agus: *Mar gheall ar lucht na mbréag agus na mionnaí bréige, ní bheidh i ndán dóibh ach a bheith go domhain i dtine shíoraí*. Ní gan fáth a deir an t-aspal: *Más ar éigean a shábhálfar an fear ionraice, cá bhfágfar an peacach agus an coirpeach a bhriseann an dlí?*
¹⁹ Agus mar gheall ar Coroticus agus a chuid coirpeach, ceannaircigh in aghaidh Chríost, cén áit a bhfeicfidh siad iad féin, fir a bhí ag roinnt thart mná baiste mar chreach i seirbhís ríocht shuarach shaolta a d'fhéadfadh imeacht i mbomaite. Mar néal toite a scaiptear leis an ghaoth, síothlóidh peacaigh fhealltacha ó radharc Dé. Na fíréin, áfach, beidh féasta go seasmhach buan acu le Críost, bhéarfaidh siad breithiúnas ar na náisiúin agus beidh smacht acu ar na ríthe mallaithe trí shaol na saol. Amen.
²⁰ Tugaim m'fhianaise os comhair Dé go dtarlóidh sé mar a d'inis sé dom, aineolach agus mar atá mé. Ní mo bhriathra féin atá curtha síos agam i Laidin, ach briathar Dé agus na n-aspal agus na bhfáithe, agus níor inis siad bréag ariamh. *An té a chreideann sábhálfar é, agus an té nach gcreideann daorfar é*. Dia a dúirt.

21 Most of all I request the servant of God who will readily respond to be the bearer of this letter, that on no account should it be withdrawn or hidden from anybody, but rather that it should be read before all the communities and even in the presence of Coroticus himself. If God inspires them that at some time or other they may come to their senses again in his regard, that they may repent, even at the last minute, of their wicked crime – murder against the brothers of the Lord – and that they may free the baptised women prisoners whom they have already captured, so that they may deserve to live to God and be made well, here and in eternity, may they have peace in the Father, and in the Son, and in the Holy Spirit. Amen.

21 Quaeso plurimum ut quicumque famulus Dei promptus fuerit ut sit gerulus litterarum harum, ut nequaquam subtrahatur uel abscondatur a nemine, sed magis potius legatur coram cunctis plebibus et praesente ipso Corotico. Quod si Deus inspirat illos 'ut quandoque Deo resipiscant', ita ut uel sero paeniteant quod tam impie gesserunt – homicida erga fratres Domini – et liberent captiuas baptizatas quas ante ceperunt, ita ut mereantur Deo uiuere et sani efficiantur hic et in aeternum. Pax Patri et Filio et Spiritui Sancto. Amen.

21 Thar aon rud eile impím ar cibé giolla Dé a gheobhaidh an spreagadh chun an litir seo a iompar, nach gcuirfear i leataobh í nó nach gceilfear í ar aon duine ach a mhalairt, go ndéanfar í a léamh i láthair na bpobal go léir agus fiú i láthair Coroticus é féin. Má spreagann Dia iad uair éigin crothán céille a bheith acu arís faoi seo, ionas go ndéanfaidh siad aithrí, fiú ar an bhomaite deireanach, faoi na coireanna danartha – dúnmharú in aghaidh bhráithre an Tiarna – agus go saorfaidh siad na mná baiste atá gafa mar phriosúnaigh acu cheana féin, ionas go mbeidh siad ábalta mairstin do Dhia agus slánú a bhaint amach anseo agus go deo, go raibh síocháin acu san Athair, sa Mhac agus sa Spiorad Naomh. Amen.

APPENDIX THREE

SCRIPTURAL QUOTATIONS

Note

Quotations in English and Irish are adapted in order to follow Patrick as closely as possible. The reader who wishes to pursue Patrick's Scriptural quotations and allusions should consult Daniel Conneely, *The Letters of Saint Patrick* (Maynooth, 1993) for a full Biblical apparatus.

CONFESSION

5. Ps 49/50:15, Tob 12:7
7. Ps 5:6, Wis 1:11, Mt 12:36
9. Sir 4:24
11. Is 32:4, 2 Cor 3:2, Sir 7:16
20. Mt 10:20
25. Rom 8:26, 1 Jn 2:1
29. Zech 2:8
38. Jer 16:19, Acts 13:47
39. Mt 8:11
40. Mt 4:19, Jer 16:16, Mt 28:19, Mk 16:15, Mt 24:14, Acts 2:17, Rom 9:25
47. Prov 10:1
48. Mt 18:7
55. Ps 54/55:23

LETTER TO THE SOLDIERS OF COROTICUS

5. Ps 118/119:126
8. Sir 34:23-24, Job 20:15-16, Heb 2:6, Mt 16;26
9. Ex 20:17, 13, 1 Jn 3:15, 14
11. Jn 4:44, Mt 12:30, Sir 34:28
14. Rom 1:32
15. Rom 12:15, 1 Cor 12:26
16. Mal 2:10
18. Mt 8:11, Rev 22:15, 1 Pet 4:18
20. Mk 16:15-16

LIST OF REFERENCES

Baus, Karl. 'Inner Life of the Church between Nicaea and Chalcedon.' In *History of the Church*, vol. 2, edited by Hubert Jedin. London, 1980.

Bieler, Ludwig. *Libri Epistolarum Sancti Patricii Episcopi Part 2*. Dublin, 1952.

———. *The Patrician Texts in the Book of Armagh*. Dublin, 1979.

———. *The Works of St Patrick, St Secundinus Hymn on St Patrick*. London: Westminster Maryland, 1953.

Blaise, Albert and Henri Chirat. *Dictionnaire Latin-Francais des auteurs Chrétiens*. Strasbourg, 1954.

Carney, James. *The Problem of St Patrick*. Dublin, 1973.

Chadwick, Nora. *The Celts*. London, 1970.

de Paor, Máire B. *Patrick: The Pilgrim Apostle of Ireland*. Dublin: Veritas, 1998.

de Pontfarcy, Yolande. 'The Historical Background to the Pilgrimage to Lough Derg.' In *The Medieval Pilgrimage to St Patrick's Purgatory*, edited by Michael Haren and Yolande de Pontfarcy. Monaghan: Clogher Historical Society, 1988.

Doherty, Charles. 'The Cult of St Patrick and the Politics of Armagh in the Seventh Century.' In *Ireland and Northern France AD 600-850*, edited by Jean-Michel Picard. Dublin, 1991.

Dronke, Peter. 'St Patrick's Reading.' *Cambridge Medieval Studies*, no. 1 (summer 1981): pp. 21-38.

Dumville, David N. *Saint Patrick AD 493-1993*. Woodbridge, 1993.

Etchingham, Colmán. Preface to *Who Was Saint Patrick?*, by E. A. Thompson. 1985. Reprint, with preface, Woodbridge, 1999.

Ewig, Eugen. 'The Missionary Work of the Latin Church.' In *History of the Church*, vol. 2, edited by Hubert Jedin. London, 1980.

Finan, Thomas. 'The Literary Genre of St Patrick's Pastoral Letters.' In *The Letters of Saint Patrick*, by Daniel Conneely. Maynooth: An Sagart, 1993.

Gaudemet, Jean. *L'Église dans l'Empire Romain IVe-Ve siècles. Tome 3.* Paris: Sirey, 1958.

Gougaud, Louis. *Christianity in Celtic Lands.* London 1932. Reprint, Dublin: Four Courts Press, 1992.

Griffe, Elie. *La Gaule Chrétienne à l'Époque Romaine.* Vol. 2, *L'Église des Gaules au Ve siècle.* Paris and Toulouse, 1957.

Herren, Michael. 'Mission and Monasticism in the *Confessio* of Patrick.' In *Sages, Saints and Storytellers: Celtic Studies in Honour of Professor James Carney,* edited by Donnchadh Ó Corráin, Liam Breathnach and Kim McCone. Maynooth: An Sagart, 1989.

Howlett, D. R. *The Book of Letters of Saint Patrick the Bishop.* Dublin: Four Courts Press, 1994.

Jelley, Harry. 'Locating the Birthplace of St Patrick.' *British Archaeology* (July 1998): pp. 10-11.

Kavanagh, Aidan. *Confirmation: Origin and Reform.* New York, 1988.

Kelly, Fergus. *A Guide to Early Irish Law.* Dublin, 1988.

Kenney, James F. *Sources for the Early History of Ireland.* Vol. 1, *Ecclesiastical.* New York, 1929.

Ladner, Gerhart B. *The Idea of Reform: Its Impact on Christian Thought and Action in the Age of the Fathers.* Cambridge, Mass: Harvard University Press, 1959.

Lathan and Howlett. *Dictionary of Medieval Latin from British Sources.* Vol. 1, D-E. British Academy, Oxford University Press, 1986.

Mulchrone, Kathleen. 'The Mission of Patricius Secundus Episcopus Scottorum.' *Irish Ecclesiastical Record,* vol. 85 (1961): p. 155-70.

Nerney, D. S. 'A Study of St Patrick's Sources.' *Irish Ecclesiastical Record,* vol. 72 (1949): pp. 497-507; vol. 73 (1950): pp. 14-26, 97-110, 265-280.

Niermeyer. *Mediae Latinitatis Lexicon Minus, Lexique Latin Médiéval – Francais/Anglais.* Leiden, 1954.

O'Donoghue, Noel Dermot. *Aristocracy of Soul: Patrick of Ireland.* London, 1987.

O'Rahilly, Thomas F. *The Two Patricks*. Dublin, 1942.

Ó Raifeartaigh, Tarlach. 'The Enigma of Saint Patrick'. In *Seanchas Ard Mhacha*, vol. 13, no. 2 (1989).

The Catholic Encyclopedia. Vol. 14. New York, 1912.

Thomas, Charles. *Christianity in Roman Britain to AD 500*. London, 1981.

Weijenborg, R. 'Deux sources grecques de la "Confessio de Patrice."' *Revue d'Histoire Ecclésiastique*, vol. 62 (1967): pp. 361-78.